PRAISE FOR *PILLAR OF SALT*

"Anna Salton Eisen shows how the trauma of Holocaust survivors influenced their children even when the parents avoided the subject for many years. A vividly colored, elegant study of family dynamics as two generations eventually came to terms with a tragic Holocaust past."

—**RICHARD BREITMAN**, distinguished professor emeritus, American University; author of *The Berlin Mission: The American Who Resisted Nazi Germany from Within*

"Anna Salton Eisen's important exploration of her Holocaust heritage is about building community, building connection, through history, through your family, through your story."

—**DEB LIU**, CEO, Ancestry.com

"It is said that Lot's wife looked back upon the destruction of Sodom and Gomorrah out of love for her family left behind, only to be transformed into a pillar of salt. Hence the title of Anna Salton Eisen's *Pillar of Salt*. This testimonial is written out of a profound love for her family lost in the Holocaust, as well as for her parents, who survived. Navigating her way through the ruins of memory, Anna bears eloquent witness to the scope of the Holocaust that continues to cast its shadow over generations. Lot's wife, however, teaches us that no one can gaze upon such devastation and come out unscathed. Nevertheless, if Anna found the courage to pen these powerful words, we must find the courage to read them and be transformed into witnesses."

—**DAVID PATTERSON**, Hillel A. Feinberg Distinguished Chair in Holocaust Studies, University of Texas at Dallas

"A true and beautiful story of a daughter's quest to understand her parents' haunted past, and to discover, in looking back, the indissoluble nature of love and family. A powerful and poignant read."

—**JENNIFER ROSNER**, author of *The Yellow Bird Sings*, a National Jewish Book Award Finalist

"Anna Salton Eisen creates a new paradigm for children of survivors to understand the Holocaust, our parents, and our own struggles. *Pillar of Salt* illumines the darkness that has surrounded us from birth. In so many ways, her story is our story."

—**RABBI KEITH STERN**, senior rabbi at Temple Beth Avodah and child of a Holocaust survivor

"Anna Salton Eisen's *Pillar of Salt* is a profoundly moving tale of generational trauma and healing between father and daughter. Through her travels with him to Poland and her relentless search through personal keepsakes and Nazi archives, she discovers her own history and in doing so grapples with questions in the hearts of all of us. Her writing is straightforward and present, effortlessly whisking the reader along for the journey into the beast of the past, to emerge into a new light."

—**JACOB WISE**, filmmaker and documentarian

PILLAR
of SALT

A DAUGHTER'S LIFE

IN THE SHADOW

OF THE HOLOCAUST

ANNA SALTON EISEN

with AARON EISEN

MANDEL VILAR PRESS

This book is typeset in Masqualero OT 12/17. The paper used in this book meets
the minimum requirements of ANSI/NISO Z39.48-1992 (R1997). ∞

Designed by Sophie Appel
Cover photo © Aleksandra / Adobe Stock

The poem "Creation" is reprinted with permission from *Jewish Action*, the magazine
of the Orthodox Union, vol. 60, no. 2 (winter 1999): 80.
The inscription on a monument in the memorial room of the Dallas Holocaust and
Human Rights Museum is reprinted with permission from the museum.

Publishers Cataloging-in-Publication Data:

Name: Eisen, Anna Salton, Author, with Eisen, Aaron
Title: Pillar of Salt: A Daughter's life in the Shadow of the Holocaust
Description: Simsbury, Connecticut, Mandel Vilar Press [2022]

Identifiers: ISBN 978-1942134-824 (pbk.)
E-ISBN 978-1942134-831 (ebook)

Subjects: Eisen, Anna Salton—Eisen, Aaron—Family
Children of Holocaust Survivors—Second Generation—United States—Biography
Travel—Jews—Poland—Tycyzn—History—20th Century
Holocaust, Jewish (1939–1945)—Influence—Personal Narrative
Classification LCC   DS134.62 E37 2022

Printed in the United States of America
22 23 24 25 26 27 28 / 9 8 7 6 5 4 3

Mandel Vilar Press
19 Oxford Court, Simsbury, Connecticut 06070
www.americasforconservation.org | www.mvpublishers.org

I dedicate this book to my parents,
George and Ruth Salton,
whose lives taught me the importance of memory,
and to my children, Aaron and Erica,
who inspired me to share this story.

"'Flee for your life! Do not look behind you
nor stop anywhere in all the plain;
flee to the mountain lest you be swept away.'. . .
[Lot's] wife peered behind him
and she became a pillar of salt."
—Genesis 19:17, 26

CONTENTS

PART 3: INTERCONNECTIONS

PILLAR
of SALT

PROLOGUE

My journey began not with a prophetic vision or a compelling call from beyond or within. No enchanted path beckoned with the promise of personal or spiritual transformation.

Instead, it began with a brief and ugly argument that I had with my father.

At the time I was an adult, already well into my twenties, and for the first time in my life I shouted at my father. We stood in the foyer of my childhood home and flung words like knives at each other. In those few moments, a lifetime of buried truths burst forth. And so began my journey, a backwards tumble into the black hole that had swallowed my father's past and left his heart broken: the Holocaust.

I was visiting Washington, DC, from my home in Texas to attend a small conference for children of Holocaust survivors. I had worked with two other children of survivors from Los Angeles and New York to organize a weekend meeting with others like us from around the country. We hoped that if we spent a few days together in a hotel conference room we might help each other understand how our parents' pasts had shaped our lives. Many of us wanted to discuss how we could use the legacy of the Holocaust as a positive influence in our lives. Some were looking to blame their parents for their own dysfunction. All of us expected to experience that special connection that exists among the children of survivors.

It was the 1990s, and as our parents reached their golden years they were drawn into a new era of Holocaust acceptance. Holocaust museums were rising up in major cities across the country. There was a flurry of academic books and personal memoirs, survivor interview projects, and films involving the Holocaust. After years of silence, it was now acceptable and even in vogue to study and speak about the Nazis' terrible crimes and to memorialize their innocent victims. And as Holocaust remembrance became an honorable obligation, the responsibility to bear witness was being passed down from our aging parents to us.

We grew up with parents whose stories and struggles as survivors of the Holocaust were unique, but we shared a common bond. Our parents had all endured similar horrors, no matter which of the twenty-one Nazi-occupied countries they were from. Their stories typically began with the German occupation of their hometowns, after which they were led into crowded and squalid ghettos and then to their doom in the concentration camps. Some fled into the forests; others were lucky enough to be hidden by righteous Gentiles. When the day of liberation finally arrived, our parents faced broken lives and uncertain futures.

They spent the first years after liberation searching for missing relatives and dreaming of joyful reunions. When they had no choice but to accept that their loved ones had perished, they connected with similarly bereft individuals, and they became family to each other. They married and had children, whom they named after their murdered parents, brothers, and sisters.

As children of survivors, we were heirs to a history and language born of the Holocaust. We had heard so many stories that we could envision the transports in the crude and crowded boxcars, the lengthy and torturous roll calls, and the selections. This bitter legacy bound us to each other and marked us as different from the rest of the world.

It was not unusual for one child in a family, like myself, to become intensely interested in our parents' Holocaust experiences, sometimes as a way to connect with our often-emotionally distant parents. We wanted to know the truth about the horrors they had endured so that we could understand the unremitting grief that we saw in their eyes.

The children of Holocaust survivors are collectively referred to as the Second Generation. Not since the biblical flood and the start of a new world with Noah had there been a second counting of generations. Our parents' entire world was destroyed and with us they had to begin anew.

After the conference ended, I went to visit my parents, George and Ruth Salton, in the suburbs of Maryland. It was a beautiful autumn day, and as I drove to the house where I spent my childhood, I saw that the leaves on the trees were changing into deep reds and bright golds. It was the time of year when school began and the Jewish holidays neared. As I came upon familiar streets and passed my old school, I was flooded with memories.

My parents were waiting for me. The front door opened and they stepped out to greet me before I reached the porch. We stood about hugging and talking until my mother ushered me towards the kitchen, where she had laid out a platter of bagels and tuna fish and my favorite rugelach pastries. A fresh pot of coffee was percolating on the counter. We sat together around the table and caught up on our lives. It was the first time I had been home to visit without my husband and children, and it was nice to have my parents to myself.

After we finished lunch, my mother began clearing the dishes and my father asked me to go outside with him just because it was such a beautiful day. As we headed towards the door, I began telling him about a Jewish genealogist that I heard about at the conference. For a few thousand dollars, this person would travel to my father's ancestral hometown in Poland and spend several days tracing and documenting our family roots. They would make us a videotape of how the town looked today and bring us photocopies of any family documents, including birth, marriage, and death certificates, that might remain in the town's municipal archives.

My father stopped me at the doorway and reacted with a surprising burst of anger. "That's ridiculous," he said. "Why would you waste your money on some silly pieces of paper that mean nothing? Everyone is dead and everything is gone and there is nothing you can do to bring anyone or anything back. Why would we care about a town that turned on us and ran us out into the hands of the Nazis?"

"Still," I said, "I could have something with our family's name on it, something to show that those people existed."

He suddenly looked very hurt and upset. He took a deep breath before he spoke. "I am Adam!" he said in a voice that shook like thunder. "Nothing came before me. Everything and everyone is gone and it all starts over with me!"

I felt my own pain and anger well up and rise from inside me. "You're not Adam!" I shouted back. "You had a family! Just because you refuse to speak of them doesn't mean they didn't exist. All I know about your mother, my grandmother that you named me after, is that she died in the gas chamber, and that isn't enough!"

For a moment, we stood speechless, looking at each other with tears in our eyes. For the first time, I wasn't just his little girl. I was an adult, standing there with my father, trying to find out the truth of his past. And suddenly I realized that his past was also my own. I went into the den and came back with a yellow legal pad and a pen. "Tell it to me," I said. "I don't know anything. Tell me the names of the people in your family. Tell me the names of the aunts and uncles and cousins who all disappeared. Tell me the names of the towns you lived in and the names of the people you knew. Tell me the names of the ten concentration camps you were in and what happened in each one. Tell me about my grandparents, not just how they died but how they lived. Tell me how it began and how it ended. For God's sake, Daddy, I need to know. Tell me what they did to you."

And so my journey began.

PART ONE

America

FRAGMENTS OF CHILDHOOD

I can't remember New York. I know that I was born in the small town of Rome in 1959 in a place known as upstate. My parents, George and Ruth, my two older brothers, Henry and Alan, and I, the baby girl Anna, lived in a tiny two-bedroom house on West Chestnut Street. After so many years my memories are like a jigsaw puzzle with missing pieces.

I can't recall the look of the house or the bend of the street, but I remember the long cold winters, when the snow drifts stood taller than my head. There was an oak tree in our backyard with a trunk so big we could not put our arms around it and have our fingertips meet. A family on one side kept their barking and unfriendly dog Blacky chained to the side of their house. I shared the big bedroom with my two brothers, and we had a modern living room sofa the color of goldenrod flowers.

We lived in New York until I was almost five years old, a happy child in a close-knit family. I spent those years playing with my brothers and clinging to my mother's skirts. I took ballet and swimming lessons and went to air shows with my brothers and father at the nearby Griffiss Air Force Base. Some of this I learned from my parents later on, and some I learned after digging through the collection of washed-out photos that my parents kept in a cardboard box deep in the back of their closet. I can put together the images of me as a little girl: smiling in a pretty white winter coat, standing with my two brothers at the edge of a lake, and sitting at a picnic table surrounded by other children as I lean over to blow out the candles on a birthday cake. But mostly what I remember from those upstate years are feelings of comfort and safety.

When I was nearly five, we moved to Maryland, after my father, an engineer who worked at the Griffiss Air Force Base, accepted a new job at the Pentagon. We left without much fanfare or long good-byes. I thought we were so happy to leave upstate because of the tough winters or the fact that we had no family there. Later, I pondered the fact that we didn't stay in touch and never visited our former neighbors and friends. I realized that that was my parents' way of surviving after the Holocaust—by not, like Lot's wife, looking back.

My parents were excited and proud to be moving to Potomac, Maryland. My father's long years of working full-time at the Griffiss Air Force Base while attending college and graduate school at night had finally paid off. Soon he would have a position in military communications at the Defense Department. We headed to Maryland like pioneers ready to conquer a new land. My mother looked forward to making friends among our new neighbors, volunteering in our classrooms, joining some of the Jewish women's organizations, and finding a synagogue for us to attend. The energy and optimism of this transition felt like the first day of school.

We lived in an apartment in Maryland for a few months until our house, still under construction, was ready. Then we moved into a brand new two-story home. For the first time, my brothers and I each had our own bedroom. My mother had chosen the Queen Anne model from the handful of home designs in our subdivision, and I took the name's similarity to mine as a good omen.

The house was a white two-story colonial with black shutters. There was a spacious finished basement that my brothers and I could play in when we had our new friends over and that I could use for birthday parties and sleepovers. Even my father got caught up in our excitement and promised to buy us a ping-pong table for the basement.

On moving day as we drove to our new house, I sat between my two brothers in the back seat and looked out the window with wonder and anticipation. We passed a long, red brick building, and my parents told me it was the new Beverly Farms Elementary School where I would begin kindergarten in a few weeks. It was constructed on the grounds of a former apple orchard and named after the farmer's daughter. We turned onto our street, Milbern Drive, and as we made our way down the long, curving road I saw lots of children playing outside on their front lawns and riding their bicycles up and down the street. This new world seemed sweet and ripe and full of promise, and I looked forward to fitting in.

During the first few days after we arrived, our house was crowded with neighbors who came to welcome us. I remember the aroma of freshly baked coffee cakes and the sounds of friendly conversations. The visitors went up and down the stairs, peering into the rooms to see how we had decorated them—our floor plan being identical to many of theirs. They complimented my mother on her choice of the harvest gold color scheme for the kitchen, and the modern shag carpeting she had selected for the children's bedrooms. They flattered her when they noticed her signature on the oil paintings that my father had begun hanging throughout the house.

It was a glorious beginning. My father mounted a plaster sculpture of an American eagle over the fireplace in our new family room and affixed a mezuzah on the door post of our glossy black front doors. This was my parents' dream come true: to live happy and free as American Jews.

My brothers and I set out to meet the other children who lived on Milbern Drive. There were kids of all ages, and within a few days we were playing at each other's houses and organizing games of tag across our lawns. I remember sitting on the front porch on those first sunny autumn days playing jacks with my new girlfriends. As the daylight faded, my brothers and I played kickball in the street with our friends.

We felt happy to be part of the neighborhood. Soon we knew which parents were the strictest—they yelled from their porches for their children to come in at dinnertime—and which parents would always welcome us inside and set an extra place for us at their table. Our neighbors were Italian and Greek and other ethnicities, but they were all born in America. We learned to appreciate the difference between homemade Italian spaghetti sauce and the canned, store-bought type, and were delighted to discover the sticky crunchy sweetness of Greek baklava fresh from the oven.

My parents had come to the United States right after the war and still spoke with thick foreign accents. My friends and some of their parents asked me where they were from. I hesitated and stumbled as I tried to explain, but I wasn't actually sure. Most of the time I simply said that they were from Europe. If that didn't end the discussion, I said that they were from all over and had lived in different countries, and I named a few in no particular order.

This was the same kind of evasive answer that I had heard my parents give. It wasn't until I was older that I realized just how ridiculous it sounded. My parents had become United States citizens and considered themselves Americans. Sometimes they told people they were from New York, and I thought they were grinning inside as they saw the confused looks they got in response. They had no desire to claim a birthright in the Europe they had left behind or with the Germans who had orchestrated the destruction of their lives and the extermination of all but a handful of their relatives. At the time I understood none of this, only that my parents sounded different when they spoke and that it made people sometimes treat us strangely and ask lots of questions we couldn't answer.

Like every child in new surroundings, I tried to fit in with the other kids. I kept to myself the growing realization that, the more I compared my family to the families of my new friends, the more I realized how different we were.

I began to challenge my parents to do things the way my friends' parents did, and took advantage of their persistent desire to become more American. I often returned from a visit to a friend's house full of new suggestions. Sadly, I never was able to convince my mother to buy the breakfast cereal with little marshmallows mixed in or the foil-wrapped chocolate snack cakes my friends packed in their lunch boxes. My mother never appreciated these modern conveniences and wouldn't cook anything that came out of a box. No macaroni and cheese or Hamburger Helper was ever served at our dinner table. My mother thought that using shortcuts and packaged foods wasn't real cooking and that all her hard work and efforts were demonstrations of her love for us and skill as a good mother. That was my mother in a nutshell. She had come of age during the Holocaust and now, as a young wife raising a family in America, she tried to be good at everything as if she had to prove herself over and over again.

There was something else about my mother. She kept a friendly distance from our neighbors, and often reminded me that friends were still strangers and not the same as family. When I had a fight with a friend, she would counsel me to move on rather than try to work it out. "You'll have other friends," she told me. "You'll learn like I did that people will come and go in your life and the only people that matter are family." I could sense, little by little, that our new life was encumbered by a past I knew nothing about.

LUCJAN SALZMAN

It was the 1960s. My girlfriends hung posters of The Monkees on their bedroom walls and strands of colorful beads over their windows instead of curtains; their bedspreads were patterned with peace signs. An antique porcelain chandelier hung in my bedroom; I had a matching white provincial bedroom set and pastel floral wallpaper that my parents had put all over the walls and ceiling. I felt like I was living in a French-castle dollhouse. My mother must have picked out what she would have chosen for herself if she had had her childhood back.

Although my parents never had any formal training in art, my father discovered his drawing abilities while in the concentration camps, where the guards forced him to create sexual illustrations for their amusement. My mother purchased a series of art books when she lived in New York and taught herself how to paint. Both parents thought of themselves as talented artists and they sought to make every inch of our home their gallery. Walls in every room and hallway displayed their oil paintings. There were scenes of European villages and ballerinas, and an occasional portrait of some Jewish figure or rabbi. They set up an easel in the basement—I could smell the pungent oil paints and turpentine when I opened the door to go downstairs and play.

On my brothers' bedroom walls they painted a series of murals. The first was a quaint European scene of sailboats on a lake. That lasted until my brother became a teenager, at which point my parents painted over it with a colorful cubist design. No surface was safe. They chopped up ceramic tiles and created mosaics of fruits on the kitchen backsplash. My mother took up sculpture, and soon our house had a bust of my father's head on a pedestal. A nude torso that she had cast in bronze presided over a corner of the living room. They kept their love of European culture, art, and music alive. They were tied to the old world, which I knew nothing about; and as I looked at the paintings of towns and rabbis, I wondered—but somehow knew not to ask—if they had been to the faraway places and known about the people they painted.

For most of my youth, I knew nothing about the Holocaust and had not even heard the word. I knew that my parents were called "survivors," but didn't really know what that meant. While my mother had relatives living in New York, including her own mother, two sisters, and a brother, my father seemed to have no parents, brothers, or sisters, though he did have some cousins in New York that we saw every few years.

There were no photographs of my parents' families anywhere in our house. I never saw a picture of my parents when they were children. They never spoke about their own childhood. They told me no stories about how they learned to ride a bike or swim, or about what they did with their friends when they were my age. It seemed like they had never been children and that their lives began only after the war, after they came to America and had my brothers and me.

I did not know what my father's parents looked like until many years later when I found a small black and white photograph in a drawer of the nightstand in my parents' bedroom. It was strange and comforting to finally see the faces of the grandparents who had died before I was born.

My grandparents appeared to be in their thirties. My grandmother's glossy, dark, and wavy hair was cut short; she wore a dress with a pattern of flowers, and around her neck, a single strand of pearls. I could see how my brother Henry resembled her. My grandfather was completely bald and looked serious in his round-rim glasses and his suit and tie. They were so young in the photograph, which made it impossible for me to imagine them as my grandparents. I was named Anna after my grandmother, and my brother Henry after my grandfather. I wondered whether it was difficult for my father to call us by the names of his parents. Once my father did tell me that, whenever he tried to remember the good things, those memories called to mind the boxcars and the death camps and his parents' terrible deaths in the gas chamber. "Better not to remember at all," he once told me.

I began to notice that my friends had big festive gatherings for Thanksgiving and other holidays, while we set only enough places at the table for my brothers, parents, and me. Occasionally, my one uncle came to visit us from New York for the Passover holiday. He spoke mostly to my mother, in Yiddish, and I didn't understand a thing they said.

My mother spent several days preparing for the Jewish holidays. The whole house was filled with the wonderful aroma of fried potato pancakes at Hanukkah, with gefilte fish at the High Holidays, and with chopped apples, nuts, and sweet wine mixed to make the haroset at Passover. Her towering sponge cakes dusted with powdered sugar, her golden apple cakes, and her flourless chocolate nut tortes were lined up on the kitchen counter. She polished our best silver, took out our finest crystal and dishes, and set a lovely table in the dining room. But a few times, right before she called everyone to the table, I walked into the kitchen and found her standing over a simmering pot of soup or one of her golden roasts, crying. She quickly wiped away her tears with the back of her hand and told me that it was the onions she'd been cutting, or she gave some other excuse; but I knew that she was missing her family and remembering the holidays before the war when her parents' home was filled with people for every occasion. When I listened to my friends complaining about how they couldn't play on a weekend because they had to go visit their grandparents or go play with their cousins, I felt envious of them and sad that my family was always so alone.

Sometimes I overheard my parents talking about the Holocaust. Though they spoke in hushed voices, I heard them mention the "camps" and the "ghettos." I realized that these were forbidden subjects, and I pretended not to notice how upset they looked if I happened to be nearby. I wondered what they kept from me that caused flickers of anguish across their faces and tears that collected in the corners of their eyes. I was curious, and eventually determined, to find out about the war, the camps, and the Nazis. I knew they also worried about developments and wars taking place in Israel. They felt deeply and desperately that there needed to be a safe haven

RUTH'S APPLE CAKE

- 3 cups of flour
- 6 green apples
- 2 cups of sugar
- 4 large eggs
- 1 cup of oil
- 1 tsp. of vanilla
- 3 tsps. of baking powder
- ½ tsp. of salt
- 3 tsps. of cinnamon

Preheat the oven to 350°.
Lightly butter and flour a tube pan.

Peel and cut the apples into chunks.
Mix in ¼ cup of the sugar and the 3 tsps. of cinnamon.

In another bowl, mix the flour, salt and baking powder and set aside.

In another bowl, whisk the oil, vanilla and the rest of the sugar.
Mix into the dry ingredients.
Add the eggs in one at a time and mix.

Pour half of the cake batter into the tube pan and top with half of the apples.
Pour on the rest of the batter and then top with the remaining apples.

Bake for 90 minutes.

and homeland for the Jews in the world. I began to think that Jews were never safe anywhere or at any time in history.

My brothers and I never spoke about the Holocaust amongst ourselves. If one of us made the mistake of bringing it up and our parents overheard us, they'd be upset with us for even wanting to talk about such terrible things. My father needed everyone to get along and be happy all the time. He couldn't bear for any of us to be sad and thought that any talk about the Holocaust could only lead to unhappiness. My father had an important job and made a good living, my mother provided us with a loving home, my brothers and I were to serve as their daily reminders that the past was over and that they had survived and put it behind them. It was our job to bring good news to the dinner table, to feel grateful and lucky and cheerful all the time. We learned that our responsibility was to keep our parents happy. And over time we learned to be just like our parents. We kept our own problems and troubles hidden behind our eyes and smiles.

One day when I was eight or nine years old, I made a life-changing discovery. We had a small den in our house that we called the Red Room. Everything in that room was red: the carpet, the leatherette sofa, and even the drapes—I think naming the room was a kind of joke, mimicking the designation of some of the rooms in the White House. I was looking for a deck of playing cards because I was hoping to get one of my brothers to play Crazy Eights with me or maybe have a contest to see who could build the biggest card house. I opened the drawer of one of the side tables by the sofa and rifled through the pile of loose playing cards, coasters, chess pieces, and art notecards that my parents had painted.

Under the pile, and not in any manner hidden, were two watercolor paintings, each slightly bigger than a legal-size piece of paper. They were painted on sheets of watercolor paper that were stiff and cracked and had turned a deep yellow with age. The edges were frayed and slightly torn. I sat on the sofa and held them in my hands. I looked at them and for a moment I couldn't breathe.

The paintings were vivid and grotesque. One was of a young man kneeling in front of a large pit in the ground. The pit was filled with human bodies piled atop each other, their arms and legs all entangled and bloodied, a spray of gunshots having pierced their faces and clothing. A large group of angry German soldiers dressed in olive uniforms stood around the pit. They wore red armbands with black swastikas on them. One soldier pointed a pistol at the head of the young man at the edge of the pit. He wore a suit and tie and an armband with the Star of David on it. You could tell that he was just about to be shot and then to fall into the pit of dead bodies. His sad and fear-filled eyes looked up out of the painting, pleading for his life. The young man's facial features and his thick black hair looked just like my father's.

The second painting was of a crowded street scene, probably in the ghetto. Tall stone walls surrounded the street, which was lined with old crumbling buildings. The dead bodies of men, women, and children were lying all over the ground; they had been shot and were covered in blood. Men and women were hanging from crude wooden gallows, their arms dangling by their sides and their eyes still open in horror. Suitcases and belongings were strewn about the streets. And all the dead people wore yellow Jewish stars on their clothing or armbands. German soldiers, some holding clubs in their hands and others with fierce-looking dogs, rushed about.

Both paintings were signed by Lucjan Salzman and dated 1946. I knew that this was the name that my father used to have before the war. The same person who had painted the walls of my brother's bedroom with murals of sailboats, who had filled the hallways of our home with paintings of ballerinas and lovely landscapes, had painted these. Worse, I realized that he must have seen these horrors with his own eyes.

For the first time in my life, I glimpsed what my father had been keeping from us. The terrible things that had been done to the Jews in Europe had been done to my father and his family. His parents and his brother were dead, just like the people he painted in the streets of the ghetto and in the pit.

I carefully put the pictures back in the drawer and said nothing about them to my parents or my brothers. I buried, with the paintings in the drawer, a terrible sadness.

For a few days, I tried to hint and raise subtle questions with my brothers about our parents and the camps, but they let me know with a glare that I had better drop the subject. I had no idea if they ever saw the watercolor paintings or exactly what they knew about my parents' past. From time to time, I would sneak back into the Red Room and pull out the watercolor pictures. Though the resemblance between the young man's features and those of my father was close, the pain that shone from their eyes was the same.

A SECRET EDUCATION

My parents' ability to speak several foreign languages in a single conversation was acquired out of necessity during the Holocaust. They could converse, argue, and curse in German, Polish, Yiddish, and Russian. My mother also knew a smattering of French and Hebrew. They used these languages when they wanted to speak to each other in front of my brothers and me, or in front of strangers in public, without being understood. If my brothers or I showed the slightest hint that we comprehended their conversation, my parents would switch seamlessly to another language.

Although I was often embarrassed by my mother's foreign accent, sometimes I asked her to speak the funny words and phrases in front of my friends, hoping it might impress them. Maybe being different could be a good thing. My parents did not encourage or teach my brothers or me to learn these languages, except for Yiddish; she used Yiddish words of affection and was willing to teach us a few phrases.

My parents wanted me to study French in high school, even though German was offered, and they could have helped me tremendously with it. I took German anyway and had to drop it when it became evident that I wasn't going to pass. At the time, it never occurred to me that my father had probably picked up German while he was a prisoner being ordered about by the German guards in the Nazi concentration camps, and that my mother had become fluent while on the run. It was obvious that I lacked their gift for languages after I switched to French and still barely passed after learning only how to count to twenty and name the days of the week.

Nevertheless, I was a model student and a pleasant child while I was in elementary school. Those were my good years. I became part of the elementary safety patrol, proudly wearing my yellow vinyl safety belt and helping younger children cross a side street on their way to and from school. I had been trained to carefully and correctly hold my arms and motion the children to cross the street or stop and wait behind me, and even more importantly, how to roll the patrol belt up so the tin badge would rest on top of the folded belt. I earned excellent grades and loved all my teachers.

I was an avid reader and flew through the books I checked out from the school and public libraries. I loved reading the series about Nurse Cherry Ames and the important decisions she made over which of her beautiful pastel colored cashmere sweaters to wear on one of her dates. I took ballet classes even though I was quite plump and gratefully gave them up when the girls with long legs and slim hips went on to toe shoes while the rest of us who weren't the right "type" were still trying to keep our heads up, tummies tucked in, and shoulders back while attempting to hold out our arms.

More than anything, I loved to draw. I didn't have my parents' talent, but I acquired their appreciation for art. Nothing felt as wonderful as sitting before a new Cinderella coloring book opened to the first page with a box of sixty-four Crayola crayons, perfectly and evenly sharpened and lined up in a brand new box.

Then middle school began and puberty hit like a dirty bomb. I began the emotional and ugly struggle to learn about myself and find out who I was, and unfortunately how different I was from the kind of girl that I wanted to be. Like many teenagers, I didn't think I had the right hair, the right body, the right friends, or the right anything. I wasn't a brain, an athlete, or one of the social types. I drifted among the various cliques, always staying on the fringes where I wasn't close enough to be pulled in or pushed away.

Meanwhile, my curiosity about the Holocaust intensified. While our class was in the library for our regular boring presentations on how to use the card catalog system or on our allotted weekly visit to check out books, I snuck around the history aisles and found the books containing information, and photographs, from the Holocaust. It turned out that the Holocaust that was whispered about in our home was a truly catastrophic event in human history.

I took out a book titled *A Girl Called Judith Strick Dribben* and read it over and over again, trying to envision and memorize all that was described. In other books I saw stark black and white photos of dead bodies, naked and in tattered striped prison uniforms, with limbs askew and eyes wide open, being bulldozed into massive piles. I didn't tell my classmates, friends, brothers, or especially my parents about my library snooping. Thus began my secret Holocaust education, which I cultivated along with a sickening feeling that I didn't understand my past. I wondered why anybody would follow that strange looking Hitler with his crazy eyes and relentless hatred of the Jews and his plot to kill every single one of them.

As I became more aware of the entire Holocaust monstrosity, I acquired a vocabulary of secret words. When the physical education teacher took a roll call as we stood huddled on the schoolyard in our drab blue gym uniforms and asked us to raise our hands when our names were called, I would flash to the photographs and descriptions of concentration camp roll calls I had seen in the library books. In my mind, I saw the prisoners standing together in the bitter cold, a shivering, terrified mass wearing striped uniforms being counted for hours on end by Nazis.

I knew what travel in a boxcar meant: the days and nights when a hundred prisoners or more were crowded together during a horrific journey in a primitive wooden cattle car, without food, water, or bathrooms. I learned about the process of selection that the prisoners endured as they entered the camps, after which some were tattooed and sent to the barracks to work until they died a few months later, and the rest were stripped naked, shaved, and immediately sent to their death in the gas chambers.

I knew about Auschwitz, Treblinka, Dachau, and the Warsaw ghetto—and that none of my friends had ever heard of any of these places. I saw photographs of the crude wooden shelves the prisoners slept on without pillows or blankets. I learned how they had to survive on rancid watery soup and meager rations of bread, which was made from flour that was sometimes mixed with sawdust. For years no one seemed to know that Jews were suffering and being murdered every hour of every day. And among these tortured souls were my relatives and my father.

I looked into the faces of the prisoners that the Nazis photographed. These victims stared out, their eyes filled with desperation and despair. Whatever normal differences and self-doubt I experienced as a teenager was magnified by the belief that I, as a child of Holocaust survivors, was separated from my peers by an unbridgeable chasm.

The deeper I delved into the Holocaust, the more I kept to myself and felt like an outsider. Living in Maryland, we were not part of a Jewish community with other survivors, and other than my brothers, I knew of no other children of survivors. My father had endured the long years of the Holocaust with the feeling that no one was aware of what was happening to him, and in my own way I also felt isolated. I was afraid of anyone finding out what I knew or that I was interested in such terrible things. And like most secrets, the longer I kept it, the greater the power it held over me.

Many days I felt distracted and depressed from the sad stories and gruesome pictures, and my schoolwork and grades suffered. I remember sitting in the vice principal's office, unable to explain why a smart girl like me wasn't applying herself in school. Although I was dying to confide in someone, I kept silent. I was even afraid to talk to my closest friends about the Holocaust for fear that they would reject me and my gloomy heritage. I became impatient with them after they whined about their parents' rules and seemingly perfect lives, and I just wanted to tell them that my father had spent three freezing winters in concentration camps without a blanket to cover himself with and that he had stuffed his worn shoes with bits of paper and rags to keep out the ice. I wanted to tell them that my mother had been imprisoned in the wilderness of Siberia, and that's why she never learned how to ride a bike. I wanted them to know that the Nazis had thrown little children into the ovens while they were still alive, and that I never met my father's parents because they had been forced into a small concrete chamber where they stood and breathed poisonous gas until they died, without even enough space to fall down.

Instead, I swallowed my secrets and lived two uncomfortable lives—the outside me and the truer, frightened inner self. And in my loneliness, I longed for the grandparents I never knew. I thought about how different our lives would be if the Holocaust had never happened. But then, I realized my parents would not have met and I would not have been born. I couldn't imagine a different and better past that would have anything to do with me.

Books became my closest and most trusted friends. I escaped my own life in the pages of books, and found characters and feelings that I could identify with. My parents introduced me to the popular and respected works of Chaim Potok. I enjoyed *The Promise* and *The Chosen*, which helped me learn about my Jewish heritage and culture. But it was Leon Uris's *Mila 18* with its account of the Warsaw Ghetto Uprising that captured my heart and attention.

I finally had my parents' approval for dipping into the forbidden Holocaust stories. I knew they wanted to protect me and feared that I might be frightened if I learned about the Nazis' brutality and murder of six million Jews. They didn't realize it, but it was too late. I was intent on finding out what had happened to my parents that had left them veiled in sadness. I began to see that even the momentary joys in our lives were tempered by the memories of loved ones who were no longer here to share in our celebrations. The people who had disappeared from my parents' world felt somehow present, and they lingered in the corners of our lives.

TEENAGE INSECURITIES

My parents worried about my brothers and me all the time. They worried that we would be too cold or too hot, that we should always have enough to eat, that we should be safe and not get hurt or sick. God forbid that we would be too cold or too hot. They wanted to know where we were going and, most importantly, when we would return home. My father became an accomplished worrier, and this was especially evident when the weekends came and my brothers or I went out for the evening. He would repeatedly go into the living room and stand and look out the front bay windows while he waited for the last child to come home. It was a big problem when one of us had not returned by the time he expected. As he paced and looked out into the dark night, his worrying spread through the house until we were all anxious for the absent sibling to return. It seemed like my father was always just a moment away from flinging open the front door and going out to find the child who was missing and might be in need of rescue. Our Maryland suburb was not a dangerous place, but in my father's view the whole universe was subject to imminent assault.

He taught me that life is unpredictable and could change on a dime. There was an immense sense of relief when the last child returned and I could hear, from any room in the house, my father firmly shut and lock the front door. For the time being, all were accounted for and safe. Roll call was over.

My mother stayed out of the living room and left the pacing to my father because she spent most of her time in what we thought was her rightful place, the kitchen. She learned to cook only after she got married, by carefully following recipes from cookbooks that she borrowed from her friends. A cherished family story was that when she roasted a chicken for the first time, she didn't know that she needed to remove from the innards the small bag filled with the throwaway parts of the chicken. Over the years, she learned to recreate the traditional Jewish dishes that her grandmother had used in her restaurant in Poland. However, my mother never kept a kosher home. After the war, she went to Israel for a few years, and was more of an ardent Zionist than an observant housewife.

Our worn Formica kitchen table was not only where our family gathered to eat; it was where my brothers and I spent time with our mother, accepting her gift of love and symbol of security: food. She prized the feeling she had when she returned from the grocery store, her car trunk stuffed with grocery bags, and was able to restock our pantry and refrigerator. Sometimes we could not even open the pantry folding doors because there were so many boxes of cereal and crackers, bags of flour and baking supplies, and jars of fruit preserves and spices.

My mother became an exceptional cook and eventually a professional caterer. She started out making and selling hors d'oeuvres in a company she called Great Beginnings, and went on to cater full receptions and parties for two hundred or more people. All of the food was prepared in our own little kitchen and stored in several freezers throughout our house. My father built shelves in the basement as my mother amassed plates, wine glasses, silverware, and serving trays for her largest parties. She developed a wonderful reputation as a caterer for her artful displays of food.

When I came home from school, I could always find my mother preparing something in the kitchen. She might be filling little Greek pastries with spinach and then folding them into perfect triangles, or baking miniature cream puffs that would later hold crab salad or fresh whipped cream depending on the occasion and the menu. I would find her in the middle of the kitchen surrounded by pots and cookbooks, standing in a cloud of flour with a spatula in her hand like a magic wand. She would stop cooking, wipe her hands on her apron, and greet me with a kiss and a taste of whatever delicacy she was preparing. The kitchen was her home in the world. There she had the power to take away hunger, solve all our problems, and then refocus her energies on creating splendid events and celebrations for other people and their families.

At dinner time we waited for my father, who came home from work every night at exactly the same time. He stopped by the hall closet to hang up his coat, then came to the kitchen to find us waiting at the table. Both of my parents had lived with constant hunger during the war. But especially for my father, eating to his own satisfaction (as the Bible says), slowly and surrounded by his family, was a symbol of freedom. His favorite meal was a good crusty loaf of fresh bread, served along with a hearty bowl of my mother's delicious barley soup.

Having all those freezers in our home filled with my mother's Viennese pastries and a global assortment of hors d'oeuvres meant that I was chubby from the time I could open the freezer door and peel away the tinfoil from a party tray. I wasn't obese, but I was fat enough to hate myself for it and drive my mother crazy with my unhappiness about my weight. I learned from my parents that hunger was a terrible thing. Dieting meant deprivation. I struggled with my weight until I was in my twenties and started running several miles a day. Better to burn off the extra calories than to feel hungry.

Eating was always the cure for any ills, physical or emotional. When we were sick, my mother gave us hot tea with wedges of lemon and plates of toast with jam, carefully arranged on trays to serve to us in her bed. When we were feeling well enough to eat more, she brought us bowls brimming with hot homemade chicken soup. My father took our temperature much too often and worried that we should get well quickly. They wanted us to be physically strong and resilient. My mother told me how she would bundle up my oldest brother, Henry, when he was just a baby and have him nap in his carriage on the porch of our home in upstate New York on sunny but brisk days to make him stronger.

As children we were provided with a traditional Jewish education. My brothers and I attended Hebrew school twice a week at a conservative synagogue and went to services on most Friday nights and Saturday mornings; but only my brothers observed their Bar Mitzvahs at age thirteen with the customary ceremonies and celebratory parties. My father never had a Bar Mitzvah or even learned to read Hebrew. Instead of a tallit, the prayer shawl a Jewish child gets at his Bar Mitzvah, my father had been given a white armband with a Star of David to wear over his clothes, as did all Jews over the age of thirteen living under Nazi occupation. His Hebrew tutoring and synagogue attendance were interrupted when, early in the war, the Nazis built a bonfire and fed it with the Torah scrolls and prayer books from the synagogue. It became forbidden and impossible to continue his studies.

At my older brother Henry's Bar Mitzvah, my father was called up to the Torah during the service and given the honor of an Aliyah, the opportunity to recite the Hebrew blessings before and after one of the Torah readings. This served as my father's own Bar Mitzvah, an emotional, private fulfillment of an honor and obligation he had been denied.

As teenagers, my brother Henry and I got braces. My brother Alan took guitar lessons and played in a rock band that practiced in our basement, making the liqueur bottles lined up on the glass shelves of our family room bar shake. I tried guitar lessons and quit after a few months, and Henry narrowly escaped being signed up for accordion lessons. No one got busted, drafted, or went to Woodstock. I had an elaborate sweet sixteen party in our basement. My mother set up long folding tables, which she covered with white linens. She used her fancy silver-plated chafing dishes and served Swedish meatballs along with all kinds of adult appetizers. It was not the kind of party or food that was popular with teenagers, and even though I was embarrassed that it didn't feel like a teen party, I knew it was the best she could offer from her heart and her kitchen. She compromised when she let me put out bowls of potato chips with store bought onion dip.

My mother always gave the best of everything to everyone else and never thought of herself. She served herself last and always took the smallest piece from the platter. She used every spare dollar to buy me whatever clothes I wanted from the teen stores at the mall, even if it meant stretching the budget beyond what my father would have approved of; or she spent money on me that she might have used to buy something for herself. She didn't want me to experience the feelings that she felt growing up: the hunger, the longing, or the despair. I was her only daughter and she would do everything in her power to give me a better life than the one she had lived herself.

As we grew older, my brothers and I continued to be bridges and ambassadors to the modern American world. My parents knew little about normal life. My father had spent most of his own childhood and adolescence in the Rzeszów ghetto, then was moved through ten concentration camps. My mother spent her teenage years and her own sweet sixteen on the run from the Nazis through Germany and Poland, finally landing in a labor camp in the forests of Siberia.

My parents did not know what to expect of us or how to handle the normal and trying behavior of spoiled and rebellious teenagers. We struggled to break away from their loving and smothering overprotectiveness in order to develop our own self-reliance and independence. At fifteen, my father lived with the realistic possibility that each day would be his last. I had no problems beyond the normal complaints about homework and peer pressure. Without confessing to any sins or crimes,

I will admit that I was more than a handful. My parents were bewildered and hurt by my emotional instability as I traveled down the thorny adolescent path. Curfews, restrictions, and boundaries must have reminded them of the harshness of life under the Germans. They believed that love and lectures would bring me to reason and to my senses. They couldn't understand why I did things that would hurt them, the people who loved me most in the world. After our confrontations and arguments, I was always left feeling guilty and ashamed. I did love them very much, but they did not understand that, for a teenager, all that matters is what affects you, not how you affect others.

I began to believe that life was randomly filled with bad things and there was no way to avoid the misery that could rain on every parade. I wanted to believe that my prayers and good deeds would keep my family and me from harm, but I also knew that good people everywhere prayed and behaved and still suffered greatly in life. From the Bible, I had learned how Job asked why terrible things happened to him, and none of his friends could give him a reason. Neither could God. All Job could do was accept that life is a crapshoot and that sometimes there are no answers.

I knew that there never was or would be an answer to the "why" of the Holocaust. Why had it happened? How was it possible for normal people to turn on and murder their fellow human beings, especially little children? Why were millions of good and innocent people, including most of my relatives, murdered? Why did the people who had the chance to stop the genocide never do so? And why did my parents, among the millions of victims, somehow survive and not the people they so desperately loved and missed?

CREEPING NAZIS

Throughout my childhood and teenage years, I had nightmares. Whatever traumatic Holocaust images and fears I had discovered and fled from during the day caught up with me at night. Alone and unprepared in the innocence of sleep, I lived out my deepest fears and anxieties. I would fall asleep and then tumble like Alice into an upside-down world of horrors, often waking with a cry and a wildly beating heart.

The worst of the nightmares were, of course, the ones that came most often. A typical dream began with a peaceful storybook scene in which my family was happy and safe and together. We gathered at our house in Maryland at the end of the day to engage in normal activities, like playing cards in the family room or laughing over a meal in our brightly lit kitchen. It all felt so real.

Suddenly, fear and panic came over us like a darkening sky before a violent storm. With a loud *bang*, the front door was kicked open. Our eyes met in terror before we bolted and rushed from room to room, looking for a place to hide—maybe the opening beneath the kitchen sink or behind the doors where my mother kept our linens. I pushed through the coats in the hall closet and hung on to the metal coat rack while pulling up my knees so that my feet could not be seen dangling.

Nazi soldiers were in the house. Their heavy boots moved across our tile floors. In angry, barking German they called for us to come out. As they searched for us, I stayed completely still, holding my breath lest I be heard. I didn't know if my parents or brothers had found a place to hide. I couldn't call out to them. No one was able to help me or hide me, nor could I help or hide anyone else. Each night, just as I could no longer hold my breath or hang from that metal bar, I woke and sat up in my bed, crying and shaking in the dark. And, just as in the dream, I couldn't call out to my parents who were sleeping just a few feet away from me down the hall.

In another recurring nightmare, instead of a helpless victim in hiding, I was our family's courageous defender. In this dream, as my parents and brothers slept peacefully in their rooms, I heard murmurs outside my bedroom window and the rustling of fallen leaves. I got up, and peering through the lace curtains into the black night, I saw SS officers in their black uniforms. They carried guns and black leather whips. Their dogs moved silently, staying close to the ground. The officers moved up our back hill, trying to hide among the branches of our weeping willow tree—the tree that I played under in the sunny days of spring.

I ran to my closet and from behind the dresses and coats pulled out a heavy machine gun. Through my open window, I pointed the gun at the black shadows. With a fierce and sudden anger, I shot round after round of bullets at these creeping

Nazis, who fell into the piles of leaves. But more soldiers rose out of the darkness and came up the hill. I panicked as I realized that, if even one Nazi soldier made it to our door, all would be lost. In my dream my parents slept peacefully, not knowing that their daughter had turned into a fearless sniper. On my young shoulders, I bore the weight of the gun and of the burden to do for my parents what no one had been able to do for them when the Nazis actually invaded. I would save them.

When I woke from such a nightmare, my room was so dark that I could not even make out the door. I got up and slowly felt my way down the hall to my parents' bedroom, still terrified as though the nightmare had not ended. I gently nudged my mother, who wordlessly shifted over to the middle so that I could lie at the edge beside her. I told her that I had had a bad dream or that I just couldn't sleep. She never asked for an explanation in the morning and seemed to assume that bad dreams were normal for a child. For many years I never told her or anyone else in my family what happened in my dreams.

I grew to hate and fear the nights. Spring storms with thunder and lightning frightened me with their booming and flashing. I surrounded myself with stuffed animals and learned to sleep with the blanket pulled over my head. I tried to fall asleep while I could still hear the television in my parents' room down the hall—if I was the last one awake I heard creaks and groans of the wood floors, and I would lie there listening for the footsteps of the invaders.

After most nights, I woke up tired and grumpy, and as bedtime approached I became increasingly anxious. I tried staying up as late as I could—another secret I kept from my parents. I knew that, if I told them, they would worry and blame themselves for letting me ask questions or read books about the Holocaust. They were determined that my brothers and I not be affected by what had happened to them. Raising us untainted and strong was, for them, a way to deny the Nazis a victory. The truth was that we inherited their trauma anyway. We kept silent to protect each other from our painful feelings, but our solitary struggles only magnified the power of the past.

In all the years that I lived at home, I never knew my father to sleep through the night. I heard him go downstairs to read or just walk around in the middle of the night. My mother told me that it was just how he was since the war. It hurt me to think that the sadness beneath the surface of his smile broke through during the lonely hours of night, when the memories he kept hidden during the day awakened. I worried about him and wondered how it must feel to carry so much pain. He never once complained of being tired or told us what kept him from a peaceful sleep. And we children never asked. We kept a pact with his silence and pretended that our feelings, worries, and questions didn't exist.

Like many children, I had a full plate of fears. Though I wasn't afraid of clowns or loud noises, I was afraid of dogs. It didn't matter whether they were strays or pets in the homes of my friends. If I was out walking in the neighborhood or riding my bike and saw a loose dog on the street, I went the other way. If I visited a friend's house, it would take hours for me to settle down and trust that their pet wouldn't turn on me. My father always warned me that if I came across a dog I should wait and make sure that it was friendly before I got near it. Of course, I made the connection between what my father experienced in the ghettos and camps and his lessons on how to survive in the world. I even thought that German Shepherds were named for how they were used by the Nazi guards.

I was afraid of being sick and distrusted doctors and dentists. In school I squinted and managed to pass the vision test even though I couldn't see the blackboard from beyond the first row. None of these fears made sense to me; I just picked up on my parents' tension when any of us was sick. I knew that in the camps the weak or the sick were culled for death during the selections. Even if we ran a slight fever, my parents put us to bed and sat by our side for hours, giving us aspirin and holding cool washcloths to our foreheads. Many times my mother sat at the edge of my bed for an entire night.

I had a terrible fear of separation. Whenever my family went to a store or a place with a large crowd, I worried that I would become separated from my parents. If I lost sight of my mother, I would panic, and nothing ever felt as comforting as when I walked by my father's side while he held my small hand firmly in his.

I remember my fear of abandonment when we lived in Rome, New York, and I was taking ballet classes at a recreation center near our home. If my mother wasn't one of the first parents to arrive at pick-up time, I started to cry and worry that I would be the last little girl left and that my mother was not coming for me. When I saw her coming up the sidewalk, laughing and smiling and wearing her soft red coat winter coat, I ran and fell into her arms, my face covered with tears as she tried to comfort and reassure me.

I had learned from their past that good-byes are, too often, forever. People can say they are leaving for a while and plan on returning and never do. There are no graves for my relatives. No bodies were recovered. Everyone just vanished. And the worst thing about not having closure is that you may be left with hope. In one situation hope can save you, and in another it can torment you. Deep in my heart there was the faint flicker of hope that, somehow, someone was still alive. Every year when we opened the door for the Prophet Elijah at Passover and prayed for his return, I secretly prayed that someone from my father's family was still alive and would find us. Maybe his brother had incredibly survived; maybe he had escaped to Russia and then was trapped with other Soviet Jews; maybe he had amnesia. Although I knew that we could never fill the hole that was left in my father's life from the loss of his family, it remained—more than anything—what I wished for.

JEWISH LESSONS

There's a custom in the Jewish religion that after a funeral the bereaved family is supposed to cover all the mirrors in the house. During the days of mourning, called the Shiva period, the mourner aims to focus on the loss of the loved one. Jewish mourning is supposed to be a lonely and sad experience. Covering the mirrors helps the mourner withdraw from the world and its demands. In our house, which always had undercurrents of mourning, we should have kept the mirrors covered all the time.

My father had a certain way of standing in front of mirrors, like the big framed mirror that hung in the entry hall of our home or the mirrored wall over the bar in our family room. To anyone who saw him, he just seemed to be standing and looking at himself. He might take out his black pocket comb and work it through his head of bold black hair. But if you knew him well enough and looked closely at him, you would see that he wasn't looking at himself at all. He seemed to be looking *through* the mirror to some distant place. I always wondered what he was thinking or what he was remembering when he stood solemn and silent in front of the mirror, a faint hint of despair across his face. When he caught me looking at him, his smile would come back along with the twinkle in his eyes that masked his pain.

It was amazing that, after all the brutality he had suffered, he hadn't turned into some kind of monster. Other parents who had never experienced anything nearly as bad seemed comparatively bitter, strict, and even unfeeling towards their spouses and children.

My father never spanked or raised a hand to us. I have never met a kinder or gentler man. He lived with a quiet modesty and grace. It was his nature to make anyone that he met feel comfortable around him and leave the encounter feeling good. He made a friend of every stranger, delivery man, neighbor, and clerk at the grocery store. I remember once driving with my father in a taxi and hearing him ask the driver how he got started driving a cab. The driver ended up sharing his ambition to one day become an opera singer; then he serenaded us with his wonderful voice. Similarly, my father learned that the young man who ran my neighborhood lawn service had started out grooming the football fields in college. My father was always interested in everyone—where they were from and what story they could share about themselves. From my father I learned that such sharing of experience sparks a connection between people. I wondered if he learned in the camps the ability to see beyond the physical. Even when he had been beaten down and dressed in filth, he saw each person as deserving of friendship and dignity.

One night in Maryland, our family was driving home from dinner. As we passed the high school, which was just a few blocks from our house, my father saw that a man was standing over a woman and beating her in a parking lot. Even though my mother, brothers, and I were in the car, my father without hesitation pulled over to the curb. He stopped the car, jumped out, and began running towards the man and woman, while waving his fists wildly in the air and shouting for the man to stop. I had never seen my father so angry. The man looked up, stopped hitting the woman, ran away, and jumped into a car that was parked nearby. The woman stood up and ran away and quickly disappeared into the night. The man, now in his car, started to drive away, but suddenly turned the car around and began driving towards my father who was alone in the parking lot. He was going to try to run down my father, who ran back to our car, and we drove off with the madman chasing us. We were all yelling and afraid, but luckily after a few blocks the man turned and drove off.

My father called the police as soon as we got home. Two officers came to our house and spoke with my parents, but since we hadn't gotten the license plate number and the woman had not called in a report, there was nothing they could do. The most important thing had already occurred. My father, the police said, had probably saved the woman's life.

I was shaken by the whole episode and the knowledge that my father could have been killed. I learned that night that my father would risk his life to save another person. It was an act of Tikkun Olam, the Jewish concept of mending the world. I knew that my father had witnessed beatings and executions, children being torn from their mothers' arms, and many other acts of cruelty inflicted by the Nazis. Neither he nor anyone else could react or condemn the perpetrators. The Nazis would inevitably kill anyone who defied them in order to condition prisoners to be compliant.

It took more than courage for my father to step in and save a life; he was able to do it because he was a free man. He showed us that there is no turning away from another human being in trouble. As Eleanor Roosevelt famously instructed in her book *You Learn By Living*, "With freedom comes responsibility."

Sometimes, the past would just slither in. I remember how we watched television together as a family many evenings after dinner. My parents sat together on the sofa and my brothers and I lined up on the floor in front of our console television, lying on our stomachs, propped up on our elbows with our chins in our hands. One of the shows we watched every week was *Hogan's Heroes*. We were two Holocaust survivors and their children watching a sitcom about Nazis. And not laughing. I kept staring at the screen, waiting for the German guards to show where they kept the Jewish inmates. The little French prisoner was very amusing, and I was glad that the two characters who portrayed the Nazis were a fat fool and an idiot wearing an eye spectacle. The absurdity of having such a show on television, even in 1965! The program never did show the Jewish prisoners, but it was bad enough to see the Germans in their uniforms with the horrible swastikas and to hear "Heil Hitler" shouted in our own family room. The actors who played the major German roles were Jewish, which added to my disgust with the show.

Sometimes, in our normal, everyday world, the Holocaust showed up like an unwelcome guest. On many occasions, when we were having a special dinner in the dining room, maybe for a Jewish holiday or Thanksgiving, after a long pause in our conversation—perhaps between dinner and dessert, while my mother was getting the apple cake out of the oven or heating up the water kettle for tea—my father told us a story. Maybe the comfort of being surrounded by family allowed him to lower the wall that kept the past from intruding. Then we got a glimpse of the town of Tyczyn, where he grew up, or of the ghetto where his family was forced to live; we might even hear a tale about someone or something that had happened in one of the concentration camps he was in. These stories always took us by surprise, and it was so hard to listen and hide my feelings. I found myself holding onto the sides of my chair as I forced back tears while trying to nod with sympathy and understanding. I didn't want him to see how upset I was because I wanted to keep hearing about what he had been through. And yet every word dug into my heart. He would tell us about someone he remembered who was a good and decent person and who died a tragic and unwarranted death; or about a small and spontaneous act of kindness from a stranger that saved my father's life. Every day and every hour were likely to be his last, he told us. He survived because of luck and circumstance, not because he was smarter or stronger than the others. It was this vulnerability and desperation that I felt when he told us one of those stories.

And then the moment passed and he slipped back into the present, clapping his hands together as my mother returned to the dining room carrying a dessert laden tray. Over tea and cake we returned to our earlier conversation, talking about school and politics. Yet, inside, my heart was wounded. I collected all the little stories and little pieces of the past that my father shared, but it was never enough for me to understand who my father was when he lived as Lucjan Salzman.

During times like this I was overwhelmed to think of what my father had been through. It was impossible to look at him, with his thick head of wavy hair, and know that he had been without hair, shaved by the guards in the camps, for all the years of his imprisonment. It was hard to think, looking at his robust build and his large hands, that he had weighed less than one hundred pounds, that he had been a walking skeleton, hungry for three years.

To see him walk, his head held high, full of pride and love for his family and his own hard-earned success, it was painful to know that this man had once labored in a stone quarry in the Flossenbürg camp and dug up graves with his bare hands at Płaszów; that he had survived ten concentration camps during three years; that he had once lived not as a free man but as a slave.

AMERICAN VALUES

In the 1970s I went to college at American University in Washington, DC. I did not want to go far away for school. By staying in the area, I could see my parents on a regular basis. Their need to know that I was always okay had not lessened over time. In fact, each time I called home or they phoned me in the dorm, I could hear their sense of relief. I was the last of their children to leave home, and I knew it was hard for them to wonder and worry about us every night once we no longer slept under their roof.

I made new friends at college, but just as in high school, almost no one knew that my parents were survivors. In a way, no one really knew me. I found an outlet for my feelings of loneliness when I began writing poems in a creative writing course I took to fill an elective slot. We spent a lot of time in class writing various forms of poetry, and I found it unexpectedly easy to express myself in a few short lines. I never gave the assignments much thought, and I didn't realize that the phrases that fell onto the page were closer to my heart than I intended.

After I wrote one poem about dreams of death, my teacher told me I had some talent, though I continually failed to apply myself. She encouraged me to share my feelings and my stories through writing and seemed genuinely interested in the kinds of things I had learned as a child of survivors. When the course was over, I got a grade of C and an unsolicited letter "To Whom It May Concern" from the teacher explaining that my grade did not accurately reflect my potential.

To satisfy my history requirement, I signed up for a class called Nazi Germany. Dr. Richard Breitman was a gifted and devoted professor and an expert on the Holocaust. I sat in his class every week taking notes as I learned about the Nazi Party. I studied the rise of Heydrich, Hess, Himmler, Eichmann, Göring, and many other officers who worked under Hitler. These educated men of the twentieth century used their expertise to orchestrate mass murder. These perpetrators were not hoodlums but engineers who organized the timetables for the trains that delivered the Jews to the camps, and architects who designed the concentration camps for slave labor and the efficient extermination of human beings.

The Nazi doctors abrogated their Hippocratic Oath to heal and do no harm by conducting medical experiments on prisoners, including pregnant women and young twins, without anesthesia. We learned about Hitler's henchmen at the Wannsee Conference, who coined the phrase "Final Solution." It was unsettling to look at photographs of these villains, with their normal middle-aged human faces, and to know that they were husbands and fathers as well as murderers. I had never heard of these evil figures before, and it seemed disloyal to the six million murdered Jews to neatly outline their names, roles, and major accomplishments. What had been a blur of feelings, photos, and my father's partial stories expanded to include the giant organizational chart of the Nazi killing machine, which nearly wiped out every Jew in Europe and persecuted many other groups as well, including the Roma, homosexuals, Jehovah's Witnesses, political opponents, the disabled, and Slavic peoples.

I wrote a term paper entitled "Human Behavior in the Concentration Camps." It was a muddled mess, a miserable attempt to try to rationalize how prisoners could survive the horrors of the camps. I read volumes about the undeserved and random beatings, the ongoing starvation, the terror and violence, and the lack of mercy and compassion from the guards who for years on end inflicted such cruelty. I checked out a stack of books from the library and tried to make sense of the academic research conducted by psychologists and psychiatrists on how victims used various psychological defense mechanisms to survive the brutality of the camps. The authors theorized that, to endure the injury and inhumanity of the camps, people like my father may have become numb. But I observed from my father's drawings and from his sad, pained eyes that the persecution was all too permanent and personal.

After I told Dr. Breitman that my father was a Holocaust survivor, he invited him to speak to our class. It would be his first time to speak in public about his Holocaust experiences. He came into the classroom one afternoon and waited cheerfully as the students took their seats. Dr. Breitman introduced him and warned the class to behave with appropriate sensitivity to the topic and to be respectful listeners. I tried to be inconspicuous when I found myself once again holding onto the sides of my desk while waiting for my father to begin. He spoke easily and with carefully measured words about how his family had lived a normal life before the war. He told us about the changes that had begun once their town of Tyczyn was occupied by the Nazis. He was sent home from school after the Nazis forbade Jewish children to attend. The Nazis imposed restrictions and curfews, beatings, arrests, and killings if a rule was violated or, very often, for no reason at all. His family and the other Jews in his town were forced to leave their homes and walk with only the belongings they could carry to a nearby town where the Nazis had established the Rzeszów ghetto. When he was only fourteen he was left behind in the ghetto while his parents were forced into boxcars and taken to what the Germans promised were abandoned farms in the Ukraine, which later turned out to be the gas chambers at the Belzec extermination camp. He had been enslaved in ten concentration camps in Germany, Poland, and France for three terrible years until his liberation by the American soldiers. Though freedom brought great joy, he faced the awful knowledge that he was alone and without a family or a certain future.

I felt like the room was spinning. My father spoke in a slow and steady voice. No one in the room made a sound and not once did my father look at me while he spoke. I wanted to run up and wrap my arms around him. Even though he spoke without emotion, his words were enough to reveal to me the shock of remembering. He spoke of everything I had longed to know, but now that the words were coming from him, I found that they were more than my heart could bear.

One student raised his hand right away when my father had finished. "Could it be," the student asked, "that the German guards who set their ferocious dogs upon the little children as they first arrived in the concentration camps were just acting out of peer pressure and shouldn't be held responsible for their actions?"

My father's face filled with anger.

"No!" he said with a look of hurt and defiance in his eyes. "You can't explain how any person can turn their vicious dog loose on a tiny child and let that child be torn to bloody bits in front of their parents and say it was peer pressure. It was cruel murder and there is and never will be any excuse for man's willingness to do that or willingness to stand by and watch while others do it!" I was proud and distraught at the same time. I could feel the pain, anger, and strength in his words and in his voice.

It was during college that I also went through my activist phase against antisemitism. Maybe it was a reaction to the Holocaust and a need to feel strong as a person and vent my anger at the silent world. I heard about the Jewish Defense League, which was organizing protests around the country. The JDL protesters would sometimes show up at rallies wearing helmets and carrying baseball bats.

I met one of the protesters from the JDL at a Washington, DC, rally in March of 1977 after Hanafi Muslims seized several buildings including the B'nai B'rith headquarters in DC. I had gone with some other students to a rally where we marched around in circles for hours chanting slogans. I made my national public debut when I appeared on the evening news standing in a downpour holding a streaked and blurry poster that said "Never Again."

My JDL contact arranged for me to go to an apartment in College Park, Maryland, near the University of Maryland, for a secret meeting, where I would be interviewed before I would be allowed to join the JDL. I showed up for the clandestine meeting and was introduced to an older white-haired man who was supposedly high up in the organization. He invited me into the living room and brought out a Hebrew prayer book. He asked me to open to any page and read for him in Hebrew to prove that I was Jewish. Finally, all my years of being forced to go to services at synagogue were about to pay off. I turned to the Kedushah prayer that we recited at worship services every Saturday morning and began to easily sing the familiar prayer.

He then asked me about my family. I told him that my father was a Holocaust survivor and also a government official with an important position at the Pentagon. That's when he told me to go back to college and stay out of trouble. "We don't want to jeopardize your father's job," he said. "Go home and leave this to the rest of us. Go make something out of your life like your father has. That's the best thing you can do for the Jewish people and the world."

I realized that my father would not have approved anyway. After the war, he had many opportunities to take revenge on a handful of Nazi soldiers or the local Poles who cooperated with the Germans. But he never did. He refused to become like his captors, and instead chose to live as a moral human being.

LENDING A HAND

After college, I got a good job in the corporate world of telecommunications. It was the 1980s. I married a wonderful young man named David, and we moved to start a new life in Texas. Of course, I went through culture shock, along with a difficult separation from my parents, which took several years and a few thousand phone calls to overcome.

David and I settled into a nice new community and spent the first few years working at our careers. When I entered my thirties, I gave up working to give birth and stay home with two healthy and beautiful children, a daughter and then a son. Even though I was busy and happy as a mother and wife, I felt lonely. I had left my family and friends and moved to a small town where I knew no one, and where there was less than a handful of Jewish families. Many of my neighbors who were also new to the area joined newcomers' and play groups that were organized by almost all of the churches. Within my small Bible Belt town, there were more than thirty churches. The nearest synagogues were at least twenty miles away. I scoured the directory in our neighborhood and found a few Jewish names. But after a few awkward phone calls, I learned that having a Jewish name meant nothing. Goldbergs and Goldmans may have had a Jew somewhere in the family tree, but only the name, not the faith, had been passed down.

Reading through a guidebook of places to visit, I found that there was a Holocaust museum in Dallas. I was still studying the Holocaust on my own and hoped to find others who shared my interest and maybe even make a friend or possibly become a volunteer. If I met Holocaust survivors and they learned about my own parents' Holocaust past, perhaps they would welcome me as one of their own.

I drove thirty miles to the Dallas Memorial Center for Holocaust Studies, tucked into the basement of the Jewish Community Center. Double doors off the main lobby opened to a flight of stairs that led down to the museum. On the walls of the stairwell was a series of framed pencil drawings. I stopped every few steps to look at each one, captivated by the stark and powerful images.

One drawing depicted a large group of concentration camp inmates huddled in a giant mass for a roll call. They wore ragged striped prison uniforms and were amassed into long rows. Their bodies were whisper thin and their faces reflected their anguish and despair. In another drawing, a long line of boxcars stood with their doors pulled open as piles of living and dead bodies tumbled to the ground. There were drawings of barbed wire fences around low, long buildings, which must have been the concentration camp barracks, and then portrait after portrait of emaciated, sad faces. I made my way slowly down the stairwell, moved and shaken by the solemn drawings. At the bottom was a closed door that led to the museum or to an open entrance on the left. After stepping through the open entrance, I found myself standing in a dark and empty boxcar.

The boxcar was old and smelled of musty wood. I stood alone in the center for a moment and then moved across the creaking wooden floor to the sides where, without thinking, I ran my hands over the worn and scratched walls. I knew I was in a place marked by great suffering and misery. Desperate mothers with their children had ridden this boxcar over railroad tracks to their death. Thousands of people had been trapped in this small space. The walls were scratched and marked by their hands. I could not walk in their shoes, but I could stand where they stood and offer my broken-hearted prayers. After a few minutes, I stepped out into the bright light of the museum.

I was warmly welcomed by the staff and volunteers. They told me about the museum and some of the programs they had to offer. I knew right away that I wanted to get involved. I signed up to become one of the museum docents who gave tours to visiting groups, and I also volunteered to speak as a child of survivors, telling of my parents' experiences when an actual Holocaust survivor wasn't available to speak. I would be trained to guide visitors through the various rooms of the museum while giving them a lesson on the Holocaust: how Hitler came to power in 1933 and the early warning signs: the boycott, the burning of the books, and Kristallnacht. I would tell them about the Evian Conference in 1938, when many countries of the world failed to change their quotas and save the desperate Jews; the tragic voyage of the *St. Louis* in 1939 when a ship carrying 936 Jewish refugees left Hamburg, sailed to Cuba, and then was refused entry and sent back to Europe; the invasion of Poland in 1939; and the movement of Jews into ghettos and concentration and death camps. The finale was liberation by the British, Russian, and American soldiers.

I was expected to cover twelve years in about one and a half hours, allowing time for questions. As I watched some of the other docents give tours, I took notes on the dates and numbers they shared so that my presentations would be true to history. I needed to undertake this assignment and become a master of the stories that had both evaded and haunted me.

The museum rooms were filled with photos and relics from the ghettos and the camps. Glass cases displayed the tattered striped uniforms worn by the prisoners, along with rusty spoons, stars of yellow fabric, identity papers, and faded photographs.

Being a docent turned out to be a meaningful but personally difficult experience. Having been raised in a home where we did not speak of these things, I was trying to sound detached while I rattled off the names of the labor and extermination camps.

I could detail the various methods by which the Nazis killed their victims: the gas vans at Chełmno, the cement gas chambers designed to look like showers, the poisonous Zyklon B pellets they dropped through the ceilings, the mobile killing squads that executed entire villages of Jews, and the pervasive beatings, hangings, and starvation.

I could cite the meager number of calories allotted to the Jews who were starving in the ghettos. I memorized the details of life in the camp barracks: the inedible food rations fed to the prisoners, the thin uniforms they wore in the snowy winters, the wooden shoes that cut their feet, the hard shelves where their near-dead bodies slept in tiers at night.

I knew about the unbelievable suffering of those who had passed through and died in the camps. I tried to explain about the "Muselmen," the walking dead whose hope and spirit died in advance of their bodies. I pressed my fingernails into the palms of my hands as I tried to keep myself from crying. I felt like I was reciting the tale of the end of the world. I found myself becoming angry with the groups of bored teenagers who yawned and giggled while I told them how the world had come undone. They would only quiet down for a short time when we sat them in the library and showed them scenes from videos shot during the liberation of the camps: the massive piles of dead bodies and the prisoners who were little more than walking skeletons.

There was a special memorial room in the museum. The walls of the small room were covered with engraved gray marble tiles. One wall held the tiles with the names of survivors and their families who had died in the Holocaust. On another wall were the names of the survivors who had died since liberation. A third wall had plaques for the righteous Gentiles who had risked their lives to save Jews, if only a single life. One tile was dedicated to the country of Denmark, which had tried to save the Jews of their country by ferrying them in small boats to Sweden.

In the center of the room was a large slab of black marble: a tomb. It was surrounded by white marble posts chained together, on top of which were engraved the names of death camps. A small memorial lamp burned at the head of the tomb. On the surface of the marble slab was engraved a poem that I read aloud to my tour groups. These words stuck in my throat, and I heard my voice break each time I read them. The last part of the inscription ran as follows:

> May this monument stand as a remembrance
> To their holy and blessed names, as if we,
> The surviving remnant,
> Had gently laid them here to rest.
> Though their anguish shall grieve us forever,
> So shall our tender memories of their beloved spirits
> Illuminate our lives and remain
> A cherished and sacred treasure in our hearts.
> May their eternal souls find comfort in our everlasting love.

No matter how many times I gave tours, standing in the memorial room only got harder as the truth and pain of the past resurfaced.

One of the first things I did after I got involved with the museum was to have the names of my father's parents and brother and the name of my mother's father engraved onto three gray marble tiles on the wall. I often stood next to their names at the end of my presentation and explained that these were my grandparents and my uncle—the first indication that I was connected personally to the terrible things conveyed in my ninety-minute lecture. I wondered if the people standing about in the memorial room could see the overwhelming pain I felt when they looked into my eyes. I ushered them back into the foyer ahead of me and took a brief moment to lay my hands across the names carved into the stone. It was my way of claiming and remembering the lost, even in this distant place in Texas, a generation removed, and a world away from their deaths.

At the museum, I heard about an enormous project by the Steven Spielberg Foundation—now the USC Shoah Foundation—to interview Holocaust survivors on video, thus creating a permanent record and proof of what they had witnessed. All the interviews would be organized into a central archive and made available for families or researchers who could access the first-hand testimonies. Those who wanted to join the project would have to go to Chicago for a three-day training and interview process, after which they would be told if they had been selected.

I traveled to Chicago with some interested friends from Texas. It was an incredible experience. I was surrounded by educated and experienced professionals who trained us to demonstrate sensitivity in recording each survivor's story. Many survivors would be speaking about their experiences for the first time. Secrets and painful memories would be revealed for the sake of history and the future of humanity. Many of the interviewer candidates were trained psychologists and social workers. A smaller group comprised children of survivors like me. I was accepted into the program, and I headed back to Texas, eager to schedule my first interview.

I will not share the name or the details of his story, but I will say that the first survivor I interviewed was gracious and kind from the moment we met. He invited me into his home for our pre-interview meeting, and we sat at his kitchen table to talk about the taping. He offered a bowl of delicious homemade chopped liver and made me a cup of hot tea. He treated me like

I was a personal guest and friend and turned the tables by trying to make me feel comfortable instead of letting me prepare
him for what we would soon undertake on camera. He had a
quiet dignity and strength about him which reminded me of my
father.

The interview went perfectly. The survivor spoke with great
clarity and authentic emotion. I didn't need to guide him through
the prescribed order of pre-war, war, liberation, and afterwards.
He had been waiting a lifetime to tell his story. At the end of
each of the interviews, any of the survivor's children who had
arranged to be a part of the taping were invited on camera to
say a few words about their parent. Typically, the adult children
would arrive at a set time after the main body of the interview
would have been completed. Before that, we posted signs for
people not to ring the doorbell and took the phones off the
hooks so there would be no interruptions during the taping.

His son arrived too early and let himself in the back door. I
heard him come in and signaled to the cameraman to stop the
taping. We took a five-minute break while I went to speak to
the son and asked that he wait in the kitchen or in another room
until we finished.

We were almost done except for the last segment when the
survivor would be given the opportunity to reflect on the Holocaust and its impact on his life. It was powerful to watch and listen as he spoke of the family he had lost. He held his head in his
hands as he wept. His shoulders shook as tears streamed down
his face. If I could have the grandfather of my dreams—decent
and kind, noble and brave—he would be like this man. I had to
stand back and allow him an interval to gain control over his

emotions. I had been trained to not touch the survivors during these sessions since they were often back in time, lost in their memories.

We finished taping and I went into the family room to speak with the son and ask if he wanted to go on camera. He had obviously overheard his father speaking and the outpouring of grief that had occurred. "Did he do okay?" he asked.

I sensed that he was slightly embarrassed that his father had broken down and wept openly during the interview. "He was incredible," I said. "I doubt if I'll ever have this kind of experience again."

It was at this moment that I received a revelation that would change my life: It should not have been me in there, receiving his story and tears. It should have been his son. And it shouldn't be some stranger interviewing my father with a carefully laid-out formula to get at his heart. It should be me. That's when I knew that I needed to go to my father and ask him to tell me what he had been through. I didn't want his story to come to me from a tape played back on my computer; I wanted to be with him when he opened his heart. I wouldn't stand back like a stranger but would reach over and hold him if his shoulders shook as he wept. If he was to be lost in his memories, at least I could be there with him.

TWO WEEKS' NOTICE

Through the synagogue I had joined, I met another woman and became close friends with her. She was a little older than I, had been married longer, and had two children who were a few years older than mine. In many ways, I looked up to her and valued her advice on raising children and on adjusting to life in Texas. She shared an interest in the Holocaust and we traveled to Chicago together for the Spielberg Foundation training and interview weekend. We were both accepted into the program and conducted interviews with Holocaust survivors.

My friend was then diagnosed with cancer. But true to her personality and character, she battled it with a powerful intellect, wise heart, and life-affirming vengeance. Out of the vast resources she amassed, she came across a woman from California who was both a psychologist and a survivor of Auschwitz. This doctor had produced a series of self-help audio tapes from her therapy practice, which were designed to help people cope with difficult life situations, including illness.

My friend wrote to this woman after hearing about her theories and strategies for facing and overcoming life's challenges.

The psychologist/survivor called and said she would soon be visiting Texas. She offered to meet with my friend and me and even speak to a group of people if we wanted to organize an informal gathering.

I offered my home as a meeting place, and in advance of the visit I arranged for my local book club to read Viktor Frankl's *Man's Search for Meaning*, which she used as the framework for her approach. We invited my book club members and some other friends to join us for what promised to be an interesting evening.

I read Frankl's book, which was divided into two parts. The first detailed his experiences in the Nazi death camps. The writing was powerful and extremely moving. It was one of the first books that I read about the camps that described in vivid detail the sorts of horrors that my father had endured.

The second part of the book was harder for me to understand and accept. Frankl's theory of logotherapy is based upon man's ability to transcend his circumstances and suffering and find meaning in his life. Although it seemed a noble and worthy philosophy—to suffer in dignity and to gain wisdom in so doing—I couldn't accept that people were necessarily capable of managing their suffering; or that, if they were able to do so, they could find meaning in being victimized. I knew that some people were broken by harsh treatment and other hardships, and I could only feel compassion for them. I thought all survivors were heroes, not just the ones who came through intact.

Around this time I was still writing poetry, almost all of it about the Holocaust. In these poems I expressed my feelings of disconnection from the past. I sent a few poems off to a handful of magazines with the hope that one might be published. After waiting several months for a reply, I finally received a small check and a copy of a magazine with one of my poems in it. I looked at the glossy page with my heartfelt words imposed over a photo of the barbed wire fence at Auschwitz that some art designer had added for effect. The words that my heart had painfully wrung lay naked on the paper. It made me sad to realize that I carried so much sorrow.

I looked forward to meeting this psychologist, who I hoped would understand my feelings and give me guidance. I was unsure if I should continue with my interrogation of the Holocaust or leave the past behind. I knew I couldn't change my father and that I couldn't heal him. But I also knew that the part of him that eluded me was lost in the Holocaust.

My friend and I invited our special guest to have dinner with us before the rest of the group arrived for our planned evening of dessert and dialogue.

The therapist was not at all what I expected. She must have been in her sixties, but her striking beauty was still apparent. She was well dressed and in fabulous physical shape. I was not surprised when she told us that she had been a dancer before the war and only became a psychologist after immigrating to the United States and realizing that she needed a profession.

She told us that she had survived the selection at Auschwitz by dancing for Josef Mengele. He was the famous Nazi doctor called the "Angel of Death" because he was among those who decided after the Jews arrived in the boxcars who was to work and who would go to the gas chambers. With the motion of his gloved hand, he pointed the men, women, and children towards life or death. The three of us sat in the dining room and over dinner shared our stories.

My friend told her about the poetry I had been writing and the poem that had just been published. They asked that I bring the magazine and some of my other poems to the table. I was caught off guard, and even though I tried to refuse, they insisted that I open myself up to them. I had rarely shared my writing with anyone. I only sent my poems to the magazine on a whim, thinking that no one I knew read such Jewish publications.

I read a few of the poems out loud. I felt uncomfortable revealing how affected I was by my father's past. Here I was, working hard to put on the face of a successful, happy suburban mom, and now they would know that I was an imposter and that, underneath, I was a sad and needy girl who still felt the pain she had felt since childhood.

Our survivor visitor listened intently as I read. She encouraged me to keep writing, and though I found her words supportive and kind, the understanding look in her eyes made me realize that she knew in her own heart the truth in my poems.

Our guests arrived and we moved into the living room. After a few moments getting coffee and filling our plates with cake and fruit, we sat in a circle and began to introduce ourselves.

The psychologist went last. She told us that she had been with her sister in Auschwitz and that she had danced to survive the selection. She even stood and did a ballet high kick to show us that she still had the grace and flexibility that had kept her from the gas chambers. Most of the people in that room had never met a Holocaust survivor. Her accent and her intensity captivated us; she held us in a spell as she took us into her past, opened our eyes, and touched our hearts with her story.

She announced to the group that I had some wonderful poetry that I was going to share. I was not expecting this, and I again tried to stammer that no one wanted to hear me read my amateur writings. Everyone hoped that I would share. I went and got the magazine and turned to the poem I had titled "Creation," about my father's claim that he was Adam. I felt my cheeks burning and my heart pounding as I read aloud and exposed my deepest feelings to this room of people, many of whom thought they knew me, but whom I had never allowed to see this side of me. Almost whispering to myself, I read these verses:

Creation
My father says he is Adam.
Nothing came before him.
No traces of a past life,
　　　his childhood,
　　　the color of his mother's hair,
　　　the color of her hand upon his cheek.
No love and pride reflected in his father's eyes.
No house, no streets, no school.

And I awoke in this life.
My doll house room and modern ways
and knew nothing of his past.
　　　The camps,
　　　the whistle of the trains,

roll call in the snow,
    the taste of moldy bread and
    watery cabbage soup.

One day
the past began to creep out from his lined face,
    his broken heart,
    wounded soul,
    dead spirit eyes.
Back down the road of bones to find
stories, pictures and traces of ash.
Weave together the pieces that still
leave gaping holes.

I stand behind my father.
Push him back.
Explain the savage scar,
    the broken teeth,
    the fear of cold,
    and loneliness.
Take me to the graves,
    down the railroad tracks and into the woods.

I can no longer hide my eyes as
you hid from our discovery of your truth.
We stumbled into our lives,
unsure how to become honorable sons and fruitful
daughters.

Not connected to the generations that came before,
    walked the last road,
    saw the end coming,
    cheated in life.

Let me know they would have loved me.
As I fall upon my knees and weep my grief.
I have room for them in my memories.
I claim them.
They will not be forgotten.
Pass them on to me dear Papa.
I am ready.

Afterwards, the room was silent. I looked around to find sad and sympathetic smiles.

Our guest broke the silence. "Anna," she asked in her heavy accent, "What question do you have for me?" She asked it in such an odd and serious voice—it was like the one we used as children when we shook the Magic 8 Ball and asked it a question. It felt like the whole meeting, the whole purpose for our coming together on this evening, was held in this moment, in the chance for me to be able to ask this stranger some question that only she could answer.

I had no time to think or prepare; I just blurted out the question that rose up from my heart. "Should I go to Poland?" I asked her.

She looked at me intently and with great kindness. "Yes," she said. "You must go to the abyss to find the answers that you seek, and only after that will you be able to find the healing and peace that you need. Go to Poland. Go back and see if you can find the pieces of the story."

The rest of the evening was an afterthought. I had been forced to reveal parts of myself that I had never intended to reveal. I felt uncomfortable and embarrassed and was relieved after the last guest left and I was once again alone.

The next morning, I called my father to tell him about my evening. I didn't tell him about the poetry reading or the weird moment when I was put on the spot as if our visitor had traveled like some fortune teller just to give me the answer to my life-defining question.

Instead, I just asked him, "Dad, what do you think about the idea of us going to Poland?" He did not hesitate for a moment. "Sure," he said. "I can call your brothers and see if they want to go too. I think I might even have enough Frequent Flyer miles to cover airline tickets for all of us and Mom too." A few hours later he called me back to say that he had spoken to my mother, my brothers, and the airlines. We were leaving for Poland in two weeks. Just like that, out of the blue. The past was now going to be set in front of me to explore and examine. My father would be my guide. This would be only the second time he had gone back to Poland since the war, the first time being a business trip during which he hesitated to visit Holocaust locations.

It turned out that I had asked the right question.

PART TWO

Poland

Locations in italics mark the sites of the ghetto and the ten concentration camps in which George Salton was a prisoner.

WARSAW

In May of 1998 I flew into Dulles Airport in Virginia, where I met up with my parents and brothers before boarding a wide-body Lufthansa jet that would fly us to Warsaw after a brief stopover in Frankfurt. We were not traveling as part of a large tour group but just as a family. My siblings and I had not traveled like this, without our own spouses and children, since we ourselves were children. But this felt different from one of our old family vacations.

It was a long flight, which turned out to be a good thing. During the first of the seven hours we were animated and talkative, busying ourselves with in-flight meals and movies. It seemed as though we might temporarily push aside the painful knowledge that would be waiting for us upon arrival. During the final hours of the flight, each of us turned inward to make mental and emotional preparations for our Polish trek ahead. As we began our descent into Warsaw, I looked out the window and I prayed that we had done the right thing by coming here.

I was apprehensive, having heard, from other children of survivors who went back to Poland, that it could be a dangerous

place for Jews, especially if the people living in our parents' former homes and towns thought we had come back to claim prop-
erty. I was warned to keep a low profile and have cash ready for
small bribes if needed.

As we gathered with our bags in the Warsaw airport, the
sound of the Polish language gave me an immediate jolt—
even though my parents still spoke it fluently. My father had
arranged for an English-speaking driver with a van to take us
across the country. We had heard that it was better to have a
Polish guide who could navigate the unmapped roads of small
towns and manage any problems we might have with locals.
Flying through Poland was not an option for us because the
Russian planes used for cross-country trips were often old and
unreliable.

Our trip would be under my father's direction, which
reminded me of my childhood. My father loved taking long
drives with no map, destination, or set route because he rel-
ished letting his instinct and feeling of freedom take over. With
opened windows, he would drive and whistle familiar songs.

However, for this trip, my father had carefully planned our
itinerary. We would begin in Warsaw, situated in east-central
Poland, then drive east through many small towns and the sites
of ghettos and concentration camps before looping up north
and heading back to Warsaw. The trip would give us a history
lesson on Poland during World War II as well as our family's
stories of life and loss. First we planned to tour the towns, empty
synagogues, and forgotten cemeteries, where we knew no one
and did not have any personal connections. Then we would visit
the childhood hometowns of both parents, where we hoped to

find something or someone from their past. Finally, we would go to the Belzec extermination camp, where the boxcars took my grandparents and others from their town. That would be the core of our trip: a solemn pilgrimage to say that we had not forgotten, that we had returned to offer prayers and farewells, since my father had not been able to provide a proper burial for his family members.

After flying all night, we arrived on a beautiful, sunny morning, and I got my first glimpse of Warsaw. It was a large and vibrant city, full of tall buildings, strange looking little cars, and crowds of people who walked the wide avenues and tree-lined streets. We checked into the Warsaw Marriott in the center of the city—we were not relegated to the ghetto. My father returned as a free man, educated and successful and with his own offspring, thus denying the ultimate victory to the Nazis.

As we set out to explore the city, we must have looked like typical tourists, especially my brothers and I in our American jean jackets and blue jeans. Of course, the video camera I hung around my neck was a dead giveaway. I wondered if the local Poles who welcomed us into their shops and cafés had any idea that we were Jews, returning after over fifty years.

That first afternoon, almost everyone we met was polite and eager to suggest tourist sites and parks to visit or direct us to bakeries that served wonderful Polish pastries. We walked just to stay awake and found a tiny bakery in one of the tunnels filled with shops that ran under the city streets. My parents were delighted when they saw the *makowiec*, long, baked pastry rolls with a dense and sweet filling of poppy seeds.

"My favorite!" my father exclaimed. This was the first of many new things I learned about my father on this trip. I was here not only to see a foreign country, but also to rediscover my father.

My father's travel guides contained descriptions of hotels, restaurants, famous gardens, and castles, as well as several concentration camps. Brochures offered day trips to the camps, some with lunch included. In Poland the Holocaust tourism industry was big business. Our driver was no novice at hosting Holocaust tours, and he had his own ideas of what places we should visit and how we should crisscross the country to fill our days in Poland. As a trained guide, he chatted and pointed out places of interest during the first few days, but over time he spoke less and listened more as my father gave us a historical and personal account of Poland. The guide realized that we had our own itinerary and we only needed him to drive us to the places my father had chosen. At first, our guide parked the car and walked with us during our explorations, but after he discerned the true purpose of our trip, he stayed behind and waited for us in the van.

The following morning, after much-needed sleep and a traditional Polish breakfast buffet of bread, meat, and cheese, we headed out for the famous Warsaw Jewish Cemetery on Okopowa Street. Located on a busy main road, the cemetery was hidden behind tall red brick walls and wide black iron gates. We let ourselves in and saw on the left a tiny caretaker's office with no one inside.

We followed the path leading towards the main grounds. The cemetery appeared to be deserted. Along the walkway was a low wall constructed from broken and jagged pieces of tombstones. The black and white marble stones faced every direction in a jumbled, broken pattern and were engraved with Hebrew and Polish names and the dates of people's births and deaths. These were gravestones that predated the Holocaust, when information about the deceased was recorded. Above this wall stood another crooked and crowded row of tall, imposing prewar tombstones under a leafy canopy of trees. The air was filled with the loud chirping of birds.

We came upon a site that would become familiar to us in Poland: a small area set aside as a memorial. A small slab wall, topped with barbed wire, formed a three-sided enclosure around a low mound of large stones. As we stepped closer, I saw that mounted on the surface of the stones were photographs of children who had been victims of the Holocaust. Little pebbles, placed as a sign of remembrance, were strewn among the stones and photographs. A small plaque read, "IN MEMORY OF ONE MIL-LION JEWISH CHILDREN MURDERED BY NAZI GERMAN BARBARIANS 1939–1945." In front of the wall and stone mound, squares of white marble had been laid in the black gravel to form a Jewish meno-rah. I stood there wondering if this was all that was left from these lives. Anger permeated my heart.

We walked over to a large, blackened statue of a man hold-ing a child in his arms while leading a group of children holding hands as they walked behind him. The face of the man showed his great pain; the child in his arms clung to him, its tiny arms wrapped around his neck. A nameplate before the statue iden-tified the man as Janusz Korczak. My father told us that he was the director at the Jewish orphanage in Warsaw, which was moved into the Warsaw ghetto after the Nazi occupation.

In August of 1942, when the Nazis came to take the Jewish children from the Warsaw orphanage to the boxcars that would transport them to the Treblinka extermination camp, Janusz Korczak refused to leave them, even though he could have remained behind and saved himself. He walked with the frightened children, who were ordered to leave the orphanage so quickly that they went without shoes and walked to the trains in their bare feet. Korczak was voluntarily deported and died with his orphans at Treblinka. He gave his life for the sake of those innocent children who could not be saved, but who were comforted by his presence. At the base of the statue, visitors had left small glass memorial candles and bouquets of flowers. The heroism and selflessness of this great man stood out in the sea of indifference that characterized the Holocaust. The sky clouded over and it began to rain.

We turned and began to silently and separately walk up the various paths that led deeper into the heavily wooded burial grounds of the Warsaw Jewish Cemetery. Going up a hilly footpath, all I could see were endless rows of tombstones amidst a thick forest of trees.

I caught sight of my parents and brothers, each wandering alone through the cemetery. Stones and yahrzeit memorial candles, some still burning, had been left at some of the graves.

I joined my parents and brothers in front of one of the symbolic unmarked graves for the victims of the Holocaust. We stood shoulder to shoulder as my father, in a deep and trembling voice, translated and read aloud the names on the tomb and an inscription about remembering those who were murdered.

As sad and forgotten as the cemetery seemed, it was also a place of quiet beauty and peace. Under the heavy and full branches of the towering trees and with the song of birds, Jews were buried here before the war.

We left the cemetery and drove to one of the few remaining synagogues in Warsaw. The Nożyk Synagogue, once a place of active religious life, was used as a warehouse and stables by the Germans. It was common for the Nazis to desecrate Jewish sites. After being restored and reopened in 1983, the synagogue held Sabbath worship services for the small population of Jews who still lived in Warsaw, as well as tourists like us who were seeking a place to pray and to find other Jews on similar journeys.

The doors of the large stone building were locked. A small sign directed us to use an entrance at the back. We went inside and walked into a beautiful two-story sanctuary.

An elderly white-haired man wearing a yarmulke came out from a side room to greet us. He spoke to my mother in Yiddish and told her that he was the gabbai, an official who helped run the synagogue. My mother translated to us that the locked front doors were recently boarded up after being firebombed by local vandals. Antisemitism was still rampant in Poland. I could make out from their conversation the names of some Polish towns and family names, and I knew that they were trying to see if they were from nearby towns or knew each other's families. I heard them exclaim something excitedly about a cousin. They had made a possible, although unlikely and impossible-to-verify, connection.

I climbed up the worn, winding wooden staircase to the women's section and stepped down to the front row to sit alone on a bench that looked down over the sanctuary. At one time, this was a sacred place of worship, a place filled with people and prayers; a community gathered here to celebrate the seasons and rhythms of Jewish life. Now it was empty and silent except for the echo of the gabbai's footsteps across the stone floor.

We left the synagogue, and our next destination was the famed Warsaw ghetto. Established by the Germans in 1942, the ghetto eventually held close to 450,000 Jews in a tiny area of approximately 1.3 miles.

Today, at the center of a plaza, is a building-size monument to the Jews of the Warsaw ghetto. In the center of this empty park square, there stands an enormous stone memorial shaped like a wall. On one side is a sculpture of people walking in a line: the Jews being forced into the ghetto and then onto the trains. There are parents clutching their little children and a lone man carrying a Torah scroll. On the other side of the wall, carved out of black stone, are the ghetto resistance fighters. A mass of bodies, of old and young men and a woman, stands strong and tall in defiance. At the bottom is a sculpted man whose head has collapsed in his arms.

We stood in the massive empty forum. It was impossible to reconcile Warsaw's Monument to Ghetto Heroes with the horror and bravery it represented. There were no photos posted to show the true horrors of this place. No recordings of the shouts, beatings, barking dogs, and brutality. There was just silence.

Left to right: Anna and her brothers, Henry and Alan, in 1964 at a lake in upstate New York. Photograph from the author's collection.

Left to right: Anna, Manek, Henry, and Lucjan Salzman (George Salton) in 1928. One of the only surviving images of the Salzman family from before the war. Photograph from the author's collection.

Left to right: Anna and Henry Salzman, the parents of George Salton, in a photo taken at an unknown date before the Holocaust. The author found this photo in a bedroom drawer, and it was the first time she had seen an image of her grandparents.

Sketch by George Salton of his final parting from his parents, Anna and Henry Salzman. In July 1942 his parents were transported from the Rzeszów ghetto to the Belzec concentration camp, where they were murdered.

Watercolor by George Salton, painted in 1946 during his time at the Neustadt displaced persons camp in Lübeck, Germany. Surrounded by Nazis and onlookers, a young Jewish man kneels before an execution pit. United States Holocaust Memorial Museum Collection, gift of George Salton.

Watercolor by George Salton, painted in 1946 while at the Neustadt displaced persons camp in Lübeck, Germany. The image depicts the liquidation of the Rzeszów ghetto in 1942. United States Holocaust Memorial Museum Collection, gift of George Salton.

Monument to the Ghetto Heroes from the Warsaw Ghetto Uprising of 1943. Anna and her family visited this memorial in 1998. Distributed under a CC-BY 2.0 license, https://creativecommons.org/licenses/by/2.0/deed.en. Photo by Fred Romero, https://www.flickr.com/photos/129231073@N06/25474215486/. No changes were made.

Umschlagplatz Monument in Warsaw, which Anna and her family visited in 1998. This site was where over 300,000 Jews from the Warsaw ghetto were deported between 1942 and 1943.

Memorial to the Victims of the Płaszów Concentration Camp. Photograph taken by Anna during her family's visit to Poland in 1998. George Salton was a prisoner at Płaszów during the Holocaust.

George Salton, in front of his boyhood home in Tyczyn, Poland, in 1998. Photograph from the author's collection.

A room inside the boyhood home of George Salton, in Tyczyn, Poland. The photograph, taken during the Salton family's visit in 1998, is from the author's collection.

Memorial statue at the Belzec Extermination Camp, where Anna's grandparents and extended family, on both sides, were murdered. Photo taken by the author in 1998.

Ruth Salton, *second from left*, with two friends during her 1946 return to Europe after her imprisonment in Siberia during the war. Photograph from the author's collection.

Self-portrait of George Salton, with prisoner number, at the Flossenbürg concentration camp in 1943. The illustration, made in 2000, is from the author's collection.

Sketch by George Salton of survivors from the Wöbbelin concentration camp on the day of liberation in 1945. From the author's collection.

Left to right: George Salton and James Magellas in 2007 at the Wöbbelin concentration camp during a memorial service marking sixty-two years since the liberation of the camp. Magellas, a decorated member of the 82nd US Army Airborne Division, was among the liberators. Photograph from the author's collection.

We drove to the Umschlagplatz, the central collection and deportation point for the Warsaw ghetto. From 1942 to 1943, 300,000 Jews were ordered to gather here with their small bundles of belongings. This was the place where families were violently assaulted and separated from each other. They were then forced by the German guards into the wooden boxcars, which took them to the camps. These events were marked only by a small white stone enclosure on the side of a busy street. It looked like a bus stop. Since it was raining again, we didn't even stop to get out of the car.

We rode a few blocks over to Złota Street, going behind a back alley to one of the last remaining parts of the ghetto wall: a section of brick, which stands over twenty feet tall. In 1940 the Nazis ordered the Jews to build the wall to imprison themselves in the overcrowded ghetto. Now the remaining length of wall stands in a forgotten alley marked only with a small map of the ghetto and a handful of tarnished plaques. Several of the original bricks were removed and taken to Yad Vashem, the World Holocaust Remembrance Center in Israel.

At our feet we saw a thin line of stones laid in the cracked asphalt that showed the original line and location of the wall. My brother Alan walked slowly and carefully, as though on a balance beam, along the line of stones. I tried but could not imagine what had happened here—how it must have been to live in the ghetto, with walls like a fortress, with no hope for survival.

We drove to the old city, which was completely leveled during the war and rebuilt from images taken from old paintings that survived. The narrow streets and plaza were crowded with tourists and street musicians. A horse-drawn carriage filled with tourists passed by. We entered a small antique shop and saw against one wall a glass case filled with Jewish relics. There were old silver mezuzahs, the decorative cases holding the special passage from Deuteronomy that were hung on the doorposts of Jewish homes. There were dozens of old spice boxes, candle sticks, and Kiddush cups once used by Jewish families on the Sabbath. I was shocked to see a large piece of torn parchment from a Torah scroll on which the delicate and lovely Hebrew letters were still clear. In Polish, the shopkeeper asked my mother if we wanted to buy something Jewish. He told my mother that the Jewish pieces were "in."

We left the shop, shocked to see how our precious religious heirlooms, stolen from our murdered people, had become trinkets for sale. I wanted to take them all from the shelves and bury them, as is done in the tradition of Genizah, when no longer usable Jewish prayer books and holy objects are buried—to rescue them from this vulgar profiteering, and from their terrible and unforgivable desecration.

KRAKÓW

Once we left Warsaw, we drove to Kraków, a beautiful old city that somehow survived the war intact. Kraków was named the new capital of Poland after the Nazis destroyed Warsaw.

Our first stop was the picturesque Old Town of Kraków, built during the sixteenth century and surrounded by stone walls. A massive stone arch opened to a village filled with shops, galleries, street merchants, and restaurants. We walked along the main avenue and then turned down a narrow cobblestone side street, where we came upon a young boy who sat on a small stool playing an accordion. He had placed a tin can by his feet and smiled in gratitude as some of the tourists dropped in a handful of coins.

We came upon a large market square, the perimeter of which was lined with charming cafés filled with tourists sitting under a rainbow of colored umbrellas. There were big clay pots all along the sidewalks filled with spring flowers in full bloom. In the center of the plaza was an expansive white tent, which housed a flea market. Inside, we walked up and down the long

aisles lined with hundreds of stalls selling local crafts and sou-
venirs to tourists.

We stopped in front of a stall filled with all kinds of porcelain and cloth dolls one might collect or buy for a little girl to
play with. I was looking for a present to give my daughter. Lined
up on a shelf along the back wall was something we had not
seen before: an entire row of wooden figurines made to resemble Jews. They stood about a foot tall and looked like replicas of
religious Jews or rabbis. These pathetic caricatures were carved
in the shapes of old, stooped-over men with long gruesome
faces and big hooked noses. Each wore a tallit, a Jewish prayer
shawl. Also for sale were tabletop knickknacks created in the
image of the old antisemitic stereotype. Who would buy one
of these to keep in their homes? Were they meant to be funny?
Had nothing changed in the past fifty years? This was a painful
reminder of the history and legacy of this country and our purpose in returning. I left the market without buying anything.

My father had planned that we would spend the night in
Kraków. After a long day of touring, he suggested that we go
for an early dinner and continue our sightseeing the next day.
In the lobby of our hotel he had come across a brochure for the
Ariel Restaurant, which claimed to be an authentic Jewish eat-
ery with nightly live Jewish music. We decided to go there for
dinner and hoped that we might meet some other Jewish trav-
elers. My mother was curious to discover what types of Jewish
food the Polish chefs would concoct.

The restaurant was located in Kazimierz, the old Jewish
quarter of the city. When we arrived we were led to a table in
a small dining room in the basement, which was dimly lit and

had a low ceiling with arched brickwork walls. A few dozen tables were crowded together and faced a beautiful and elaborate brass bar at the front of the room. After my eyes adjusted to the darkness of the cellar I could make out the writing on a large plaque that hung above our table: "This room dedicated to the memory of Famous Polish Rabbis." On the walls were hung a series of large plaster moldings shaped with the faces and in the garb of rabbis. Under each one was the name of a Polish rabbi who had perished in the Holocaust. The waiter brought us menus and placed on our table a basket of matzoh, the traditional unleavened bread eaten by Jews during Passover. It was stale and obviously served as part of the Jewish theme. Almost every dish listed on the menu had a name that began with the words "Jewish" or "Israeli." The whole dining experience was unfolding like a gimmick that capitalized on vanished Jews, much like the wooden dolls in the flea market.

A group of musicians appeared at the front of the room, and one of them announced that they would play for us. They welcomed everyone to join in singing or even dancing amidst the crowded tables. The men were wearing black suits, and two of them were wearing ridiculously tall black top hats to mimic those worn by Orthodox Jews, as well as long white scarves with fringes at the bottoms, which looked like prayer shawls.

They began to play some fast-paced and energetic melodies reminiscent of Jewish Klezmer music, which originated in Eastern Europe. A few couples from the tables around the room got up to dance. At one part of the song, the lead singer, a large man dressed in one of the Jewish costumes, raised his hands in the air and kept shouting a familiar Yiddish saying, "Oy Vey!"

From behind him, a woman came forward, dancing about while holding a large menorah, the Jewish candelabra lit at Hanukkah, its candles burning brightly in the darkness. Many people were now dancing; one man, seemingly very drunk, danced wildly with a bottle of wine. Everyone in the room clapped their hands along with the music, and when the song ended there was much applause and whistling. My mother got up from our table and went to speak with one of the musicians. When she returned, she told us that they weren't Jews but Ukrainians and that this was all part of their popular Jewish act.

When history and memories end up in the wrong hands, this is what can happen. I left the restaurant feeling disgusted and hurt.

In the morning, we returned to the Jewish section of Kraków to visit the Old Synagogue, one of the synagogues that survived the war. The building stood at the end of the street. Even without a sign, we knew it was a synagogue. The bricks around the windows and in the walls had been shaped into traditional arches to resemble the tablets on which the Ten Commandments were given to the Israelites at Mount Sinai. A small plaque in the entry said that the large sanctuary was partially destroyed but had been rebuilt and that the synagogue was only open as a museum.

We walked into a small foyer that led into a tall, airy sanctuary. Several large and impressive chandeliers hung from the ceiling. The room had tremendous stone columns and a raised pulpit in the center, which was enclosed and topped with a delicate wrought iron dome. The walls were lined with glass display cases filled with authentic religious artifacts that were recovered after the war. On one wall stood the ark, which had at one time housed the Torah scrolls. The large rectangular opening was cut into the wall, surrounded by ornately carved stone and covered with an embroidered curtain. The steps that led up to the ark were closed off with a heavy chain.

I walked around the room, slowly peering into each of the glass cases and reading the descriptions in front of each item. There were elegant antique menorahs, candlesticks, and rimonim, the silver ornaments that adorn the wooden handles of the rollers that hold the Torah scrolls. There were old and faded prayer caps, hats, and prayer shawls, or tallithim, worn by the religious men. Other cases held rare carved boxes that had once been used to hold an etrog, the lemon-like fruit used symbolically during the Jewish festival of Sukkot. There were oblong cases holing scrolls of parchment inscribed in Hebrew with the story of Esther, which is read during the Jewish holiday of Purim.

In one display, a lone prayer book dating back to 1786 was laid open to the Kaddish prayer, which is recited at every worship service and as a mourner's prayer for the dead. Someone must have known to leave the prayer book open to that exact page and exact prayer for any Jews that would return and stand in this spot. I quietly recited the prayer and thought of all the Jews who had once lived in this community and been a part of this synagogue. Now, all that was left were museum relics. As I went to leave the sanctuary, I passed a large case that held an opened Torah scroll. I couldn't bear to look at it, sitting frozen behind glass, never again to be read from, carried, or touched. I thought about Simhat Torah, the Jewish holiday when we

celebrate and commemorate the receiving of the Ten Commandments by joyously dancing with our holy Torah in our
arms.

We checked out of our hotel the next day, and as we made
our way out of Kraków we decided to drive by the site of the
Płaszów concentration camp, made famous by the movie *Schindler's List*. We heard that the camp had been demolished and all
that remained was a memorial built after the war. The weather
looked a little threatening that morning, but we decided to make
a short stop there since my father had once been a prisoner at
that location.

Płaszów was the second of the ten camps he had been in
during the three years he was imprisoned by the Nazis. At
Płaszów he had worn the striped prison uniform of the concentration camp inmates, slept on the bare wooden shelves in
the barracks, stood for long roll calls, and nearly starved on the
flimsy rations of rotting food. Here he had suffered under the
brutality of the Nazis and watched as his friends died from executions, beatings, and starvation. Worst of all was the work he
had been forced to do there. He had to dig up the remains of the
dead with his bare hands, as the Nazis had built the Płaszów concentration camp on what had been a massive Jewish cemetery.

We parked at the bottom of a large, grassy hill near where
the main camp had once stood. As far as I could see, the area was
empty and barren except for a tremendous stone monument
that stood in the distance. It was as tall as a building. I could
make out the form of six figures, lined up and standing together
with their arms extended downwards by their sides, their hands
clenched into fists. Between their shoulders and their formless

faces a wide expanse of stone had been cut out, exposing the gray sky overhead. The top of the monument, marked off by their bowed heads, cut across in a sharp and straight line. They had the stance not of free men, but of slaves.

We left the car on the deserted road and walked the short distance to a long and winding gravel path leading up to the monument. Near the top of the path, wide stone steps led to the foot of the pillar. Now the wind was blowing stronger, so my brothers each took one of my father's arms as they made their way up the path. I stayed behind for a moment with my mother while I took out my video camera and prepared to make a recording of our visit. When I looked up at my father and brothers, I was reminded of a similar sight from the past. The three of them were walking the same way my parents had walked—on either side and with arms linked—each of my brothers up the synagogue aisle to the bimah to become a Bar Mitzvah. And now my brothers supported my father in the same way, showing their love and devotion as they climbed that hill.

When they reached the top, my father walked to the side of the monument. He stood with his shoulders slumped as he raised his hands and placed them high upon the rough stone. For a moment, I looked upon a grief so painful and private that I had to turn off my camera and turn away.

We then walked over to a small memorial stone that had been placed in the middle of the empty field. We stood by my father as he translated the words on a plaque mounted on the stone. It told of the tens of thousands of Jews from Poland and Hungary who were murdered at Płaszów from 1943 to 1945. It said that the names were not known of those who were killed there but that they were known by one name, Jews. It said that in this place, terrible crimes were committed whose barbarity could not be described by the language of human beings. The plaque said it was placed in memory of those whose last out-cry of terror became the quiet of today's former cemetery, the Płaszów concentration camp.

We returned to the car and, in the sad silence that we had grown accustomed to, left Kraków to journey deeper into Poland.

AUSCHWITZ

Auschwitz. The name of this notorious concentration and death camp has come to symbolize the genocide of European Jewry. In the hierarchy of the Holocaust, Auschwitz stands at the top. Here more prisoners were murdered than at any other Nazi location; here they received the infamous tattoos on their forearms, which became the recognizable mark of a Holocaust survivor. The psychologist who came to my house was a survivor of Auschwitz, as was Viktor Frankl, Primo Levi, Elie Wiesel, and the numerous other writers whose accounts introduced me to the Holocaust. Auschwitz was the embodiment of my nightmares and of the monstrosities I covertly studied as a child.

Auschwitz, fortunately or unfortunately, remains the contemporary center of the Polish Holocaust "experience." My father was not imprisoned at Auschwitz, but we went there because we wanted to see everything that could make our trip as meaningful as possible. As we anticipated the difficult day ahead, we were quiet and somber at breakfast. The main camp at Auschwitz was just a few miles away from our hotel. When we arrived, the lot was already filled with cars and tour buses.

Guides, who carried little colored flags, formed several large groups of tourists into orderly lines and led them into the camp.

My mother took my father's hand and started towards the camp entrance, followed by my brothers and me. Our private and intensely serious demeanor distinguished us from the chatty groups whose ninety-minute interlude at Auschwitz was but a sad field trip during an otherwise lively day. At the entrance we were held up behind one of the big groups of eager tourists, juggling their video equipment and cameras. A woman next to me began eating a pastry she took out of a small paper sack. The sun was shining and the air was filled with the sounds of cheerful voices and even laughter. A sense of dread came over me, for I knew that I would not be able to shield my eyes or my heart once I passed through the gates of the camp.

After we entered the camp, we were invited to join a large group. I looked up and saw the famous words "Arbeit Macht Frei" (Work Will Make You Free) on a steel banner that hung over the gates. This was the first lie that welcomed prisoners into Auschwitz: the Nazis knew that all who entered would never survive.

Our guide was a young German, a historian who had been asked to step away from his research duties and lead tours, as the camp was very busy that day. He told us that Auschwitz was built first as a camp for Poles and Christians; later, when it was decided to imprison and exterminate the Jews of Europe, the death camp Birkenau, a subcamp of Auschwitz, was built some two kilometers away. We would go there after seeing Auschwitz.

The streets were lined with brick buildings, all of a similar size and rectangular shape. We entered one of the buildings, each of which was labeled a "block." The first one we went into had been turned into a museum. In the entry stood a twisted metal sculpture of a prisoner stooped over. Next to it was a stand holding an urn filled with human ashes. Our guide told us that all of Auschwitz and Birkenau was a graveyard and that we should remember that, with every step we took, we would be walking on human ashes.

He led us through the rooms in the building, filled with the remains of Auschwitz-Birkenau. In the first room, we came upon a terrible sight. Inside a display case that ran along the room was a giant mound of human hair—strands long and short and of every color, piled almost to the ceiling; in one area, some-one had carefully laid out a row of braids. In another room, we found a mountain of shoes, worn and mismatched and of all different sizes and colors. There were little children's shoes with tiny buttons and laces mixed up with men's leather boots and delicate ladies' pumps. Other display cases were filled with eye spectacles, artificial limbs, and crutches. Another room had a tremendous stack of suitcases—old brown and black leather cases, many with the names of families and their towns still painted on them in large letters. I tried to read all the names, which were roughly marked on the suitcases, looking for my father's town or family. Finally, we came to a room filled with clothes from the youngest victims. There were worn and faded little sweaters, infant clothes, blankets, and booties.

The sun shone brightly as our group walked outside into a courtyard with a small rock wall at the far end. At the base of the wall, visitors had laid bouquets of flowers and lit memorial candles. Our guide told us that this was called the Wall of Execution. I stepped forward and took my mother towards the wall. We touched it with our hands. We were both crying. Thousands of people had been murdered beneath our feet.

We stopped in front of a building named Block 10, also known as the Block of Death. The guide told us that this building was the site of gruesome medical experiments conducted on children, especially twins. Without emotion, our guide recited numbers and facts about the execution—in all sorts of unimaginable and terrible ways—of thousands of prisoners.

After entering Block 10, we followed our guide down the long halls, which were lined with execution chambers. At the basement level at the end of the hall was a room filled with small brick stalls barely large enough for one person. Each one had a small opening in the floor. "Into these cement stalls," said our guide, "prisoners were forced to crawl and stand upright until they died without enough space to fall down."

It had been less than an hour, and many of the people in our group were visibly upset. My father walked alone, shaking his head in disgust at every new abomination. He offered commentary during the tour guide's presentation, making clear his strong reactions to everything he saw. "This was murder; they murdered a whole people. How could they do this?" he asked, continuing to talk aloud. The rest of us silently followed our guide past a row of gallows, and he showed us where the camp orchestra played as people were hanged.

We came to a building with a short, sloping cement walk that led down to a metal door. This was the gas chamber and crematorium. The group grew silent. The metal door led to a large room where the prisoners were made to undress. Beyond were several smaller concrete rooms, the gas chambers themselves. Our guide directed us to look up to see the openings in the ceilings through which the Zyklon-B poison pellets were dropped in by the Nazi executioners. The gas chambers had heavy metal doors with little glass peepholes for the guards to look through as hundreds of people were crowded together and gassed. It was a horrible, slow, and painful death. He said that afterwards the guards would remove the bodies, many of them still clutching the hands of their loved ones.

Beyond the gas chambers were the rooms filled with ovens. Many of the ovens stood with their doors open, still filled with human ashes. I took out of my purse a Jewish yahrzeit memorial candle that I had brought from Texas and set it among the other candles left by the ovens. I lit it and wept as I recited the Mourner's Kaddish. I wondered how my one prayer could suffice for so many murdered and innocent Jewish souls.

We left the main camp and drove the short distance to Auschwitz-Birkenau. We stood outside the entrance to the camp near the tunnel through which the trains arrived. Slowly we walked into the camp along the railroad tracks that carried the trains, their boxcars full of Jews from the ghettos and towns all over Europe. In the place where we now stood, thousands upon thousands—eventually more than one and one half million Jews—were marched to the gas chambers, killed, and then burned in the massive ovens.

Our guide explained the process by which the Jews were brought into the camp. When they arrived, the Nazi guards

ordered them out of the boxcars with much shouting and brutality. Prisoners in striped uniforms carried off the bodies of
those who had died in the boxcars. Other camp inmates helped
the confused and frightened passengers into long lines, which
now separated the men from the women and children. The infamous Dr. Mengele or one of the other Nazi officers decided who
would live and who would die. Pregnant women, mothers with
their little children, children separated from their parents, and
the elderly were condemned. The able-bodied men and some of
the younger and stronger women were sent to work.

We continued to walk between double fences of electrified
barbed wire. Our guide took us into a barrack that housed a
latrine. The building was constructed from a prefabricated
wooden horse barn that had been brought to Poland from Germany. Inside, there were narrow cement benches that ran the
length of the building and were covered with a double row of
crude holes. Here, the prisoners went to the bathroom without
privacy, dignity, or means of sanitation. Thus began the transformation from being regarded as humans to being treated like
animals.

The tour was over. Our guide told us that we could continue
to walk through the camp on our own. The group we had accom-
panied headed back to their buses. We decided to stay. We followed the train tracks along the dirt and gravel road deeper
into the camp. The camp was divided into different sections for
men, women, and children. My brother Henry led us through
an open gate towards endless rows of barracks. He read to us
from a sign that this section was made from bricks taken from a

nearby town that was destroyed, and that the Jews were forced to build these barracks.

We returned to the main road in the camp. One direction led deeper into the camp and to the crematoriums and the other back to the parking lot. My father said he would wait for us here. He said that his feet were bothering him and he had done enough walking for the day. I knew that he was fit enough to climb a mountain and that it was his heart that could not take anymore. My brother Henry decided to stay with my parents. They said they didn't mind if my brother Alan and I walked around for a while before we left. Alan and I agreed that we had come too far to turn back now.

We walked towards the gas chambers and crematoriums. A section of the crematoriums was blown up by Jewish prisoners in a final uprising against the Germans. All that remained was a mangled mass of bricks and the remnants of the stone steps. I took out of my purse another token of remembrance, a red silk rose given to me by my friend Julie, an artist whose mother was a prisoner here. Julie had written the names of all her relatives that died in Auschwitz and the Holocaust on the silk petals of the rose and asked me to find a place to leave it. I carefully climbed down by the pile of stones and twisted metal and wrapped the stem of the rose around a strand of barbed wire.

We came to an unbelievable sight. On the ground were several large mounds with hundreds of metal spoons. These massive piles were covered with large stretches of chicken wire. The spoons, all bent, blackened, and rusty, must have belonged to the prisoners. These spoons were crucial for survival, for without a bowl or a spoon the prisoners were given no soup.

My brother and I walked farther into the camp and came to a large cluster of trees. Mounted on one of the trees was a photograph that I had seen before. It showed the arrival at the Gypsy family camp (Zigeunerfamilienlager) in Auschwitz II-Birkenau of a group of Romani, Sinti, and Lalleri, among them many children. In the picture, they are standing in front of this exact group of trees. They were imprisoned in this part of the camp, and it is only here, deep in the camp, on a little sign, that the 20,000 murdered German and Austrian Romani, Sinti, and Lalleri are remembered.

My brother and I decided to head back. Our parents would worry if we were gone much longer. It was already late in the afternoon and a light drizzle had begun to fall. We were walking down a grassy path between rows of barracks when Alan said we should turn back and follow the long route we had taken earlier. However, the path soon ended and we found ourselves walking in waist-high grass. A few bees buzzed around my head and I brushed them away. But as they flew around my hair, I began to run through the tall grass waving my arms around, yelling for my brother to help me while I tried to swat the bees away. I must have looked like a madwoman running and shrieking through the camp. It seemed fitting, after seeing Auschwitz, to go mad.

My brother decided that, to get to the road that would take us back to our parents, we would have to crawl under the barbed wire fence. He stopped at a spot where the space between the ground and the barbed wire seemed tall enough to slide through. "I can't believe I'm doing this," he said. The wire tore his shirt as he made his way under. I kept telling him not to crawl beneath. I could see that he was very anxious, so I was immensely relieved to see that the rusty wire had not cut his skin. I wanted to look for a safer spot and went only a few steps farther before I found a door-sized opening in the fence. I stepped through and called out to my brother. He looked at me with disbelief when he saw that I had found an opening.

Our parents and Henry were waiting for us by the entrance. As we drove back to the hotel feeling completely drained, I thought that there could be no place more desolate than Auschwitz. I thought of the prisoners who woke there each morning and had to face another day.

RZESZÓW

Until now, our Poland journey had taken us to concentration camps and towns that were integral to the larger Holocaust experience, but not necessarily to my parents' past. Now we began our descent into the Poland of my father's horrific youth.

The morning after our visit to Auschwitz we met for another robust Polish breakfast before heading east on a two-hour drive to Rzeszów, the large city near my father's hometown of Tyczyn. On the early part of our trip, I listened as my father told us the history of each place we visited. He had a passion for history and had spent many years studying the Holocaust. Even though the stories were upsetting, in most places he spoke of "the Jews that had been there." Now he spoke about himself and his own family.

In the nearly forgotten years of my father's childhood, Rzeszów was a place that he loved to visit. It offered an exciting escape from his small town of Tyczyn; there was a movie theater, big restaurants and hotels, and even a Jewish tennis club. My father had many relatives in Rzeszów and he had fond memories of spending Jewish holidays in festive dining rooms surrounded by love and warmth. Yet not a single close relative of his from Rzeszów survived the war.

My grandfather Henry, a lawyer, practiced in the court in Rzeszów. In that town my father's older brother, Manek, attended high school. It was the home of Uncle Kalman, my father's favorite uncle, whom he visited on weekends and holidays. Alas, it is also the place where the Nazis established the ghetto in which my father and his family were confined. The Jews of Tyczyn walked many miles to the ghetto while carrying their few belongings. Their Polish friends and neighbors lined the streets, calling out insults as they were expelled from their town.

As before the war, Rzeszów endured as a big and bustling city. We parked downtown near the city hall and walked down the streets lined with shops and eateries. I saw the now familiar Polish word "Antyki" outside a store and knew they sold the remnants of the Jewish life that had once flourished here. We didn't go inside. In Warsaw, my mother and I at first entered these kinds of antique shops, feeling awkward as we hinted to the shopkeeper that we wanted to see Jewish items. A few of the shopkeepers would come out from behind the counters, close the shutters, and lock the doors before they opened some hidden drawer or cabinet and pulled out a cache of Jewish objects. The Antiquities Law in Poland made it illegal to take anything out of the country from before 1945. This didn't seem to bother the antique or flea market dealers, who were discreet but willing to make a large sum of money selling treasures of the past. For a tarnished old Kiddush cup or a silver spice box that was once in the hands of a Jewish family, they were asking five hundred American dollars.

My father led us down a narrow street, looking for the home of one of his boyhood friends, Julek Schipper, who had been with my father through all ten concentration camps. After so many years, my father never expected to be standing in front of his friend's house, which he had visited so many times as a child. Now, the home was deserted and run down. The doors and windows were boarded up. We stood close to my father, enveloped in the shadow of his sadness while he told us about his dear friend and how their childhoods had ended once the Germans came. He was lost in his memories and in the immense longing of this unexpected moment.

The Germans had begun to establish the Rzeszów ghetto by 1941. Like other ghettos, this one was constructed in an old, run-down part of the city, and it quickly became an overcrowded, walled-in quarter filled with great hunger, fear, sickness, and misery. Living in a room with several other families, my father slept on the floor on a bare mattress and tried, day and night, to avoid the Nazis. No Jew was safe in the ghetto.

We came to a large and overgrown square bordered with park benches and followed my father, who left the sidewalk and went to stand in the tall grass. He told us that the ghetto was divided into two parts, called the small and the large. The Jews in the larger part of the ghetto were told they would be taken by train to work on Ukrainian farms. But because my father had received a mark on his Kennkarte, a German-issued identity card, he was ordered to remain behind in the smaller part of the ghetto, as was his brother, Manek.

Once he and Manek had the special mark on their Kenn-karten, they knew they faced separation from their parents. Their final farewell was heartrending: the last look, the last embrace, the last words of his parents as they gave up their sons—without knowing if it was safer to stay behind in the small ghetto or be deported on the trains.

The ghetto was liquidated when the Jews in the larger part, including his parents, were sent on boxcars to be murdered in the gas chambers of Belzec, one of six Nazi death camps estab-lished throughout Europe that were built to carry out "The Final Solution," the Nazi term for the mass murder of Euro-pean Jews. The remaining few hundred Jews were kept behind in the small section of the ghetto to provide slave labor for Daimler-Benz. My father was assigned to a forced labor group that he remained part of through all ten concentration camps: Reichshof, Płaszów, Wieliczka, Flossenbürg, Urbès, Sachsen-hausen, Watenstedt, Braunschweig, Ravensbrück, and Wöb-belin. The concentration camps included major camps and subcamps, transit camps and forced labor camps. As the Nazis moved the Daimler-Benz munitions factory and its prisoners to stay ahead of the invading Allies, my father was transported in boxcars all across Poland, Germany, and France for three years until he was liberated by the Americans. My father would be one of the youngest prisoners of his labor group and among only a few who were still alive by the time of liberation.

A small sign said that we were at "The Place of the Victims of the Ghetto." The Jews left behind were brought to this spot for selections. My father recalled the long hours filled with fear and beatings as the Nazis made them line up, crouch, and jump up and down to see who was fit. He told us of his own desperation and then relief when his brother and he both passed the selection, which would allow them to stay together. The square was now a park with people sitting on benches and children running about. No one seemed to know or care that the ground they frolicked on was once wet with the tears and blood of Jews.

My father took us down an alley behind the building and showed us a small yard that was once the site of the Rzeszów Jewish cemetery. He told us that the cemetery was destroyed by the Germans and turned into the Umschlagplatz, the collection and deportation center for the larger portion of the Rzeszów ghetto. We stood before a small memorial dedicated to the Russian soldiers who fought there. There was no mention of the Jews or what happened to them in that place. In the end, all but a few hundred young men, including my father and his brother, were sent to the Belzec death camp. Among them were my grandparents, Henry and Anna Salzman. May their memory be a blessing.

We came to a famous synagogue of Rzeszów. A sign said that the Old Town Synagogue was built in the sixteenth to seventeenth centuries, burned down in 1944, and reconstructed from 1958 through 1968, and that it now served as the Office of Public Archives. Our Polish guide suggested that we visit the archives and look for records of my grandfather's law practice or other family certificates of birth, death, or marriage. He warned us that the archive workers were not very friendly or helpful to the Jews who came looking for records and often charged exorbitant fees to make copies of any documents. Although the sign on the door said the archives were open, the door was locked and no one answered the bell. We had hoped for so much, yet the day had come and we had no choice but to accept our disappointment. My father was back in Rzeszów, but most of his past would remain sealed off.

My father led us down several side streets, hoping to find the house of his cousins, the Biermans. When he couldn't find it he became visibly upset. We then came to the high school where my father's brother went to school. My brother Alan looked in the front doors and windows. The building was closed and was no longer a school. All my father had left were memories, and now they had failed him because everything was different and he could not find his bearings. As we walked on, he suddenly realized that we were on the last street that was part of the Rzeszów ghetto.

We stopped before a small apartment building. My father looked up and pointed to a window with a delicate lace curtain and told us that this was where his father's brother, Uncle Kalman, once lived. Inside the building my father spoke to a man behind the counter of a small newspaper and cigarette kiosk in the lobby. Then we went up the stairs to an apartment on the first-floor landing. "This is the door," my father said. "I remember coming here to visit. I remember standing in this spot and walking through this door." We stood there, uncertain what to say or do. My father didn't knock on the shabby door, but just stood and held his head in his hands. His excitement turned to dejection before he turned and led us back down the stairs and out onto the street.

We walked down a cobblestone street that led to an older, quaint part of the city. My father seemed to know his way around and brought us to a large building painted a bright yellow gold that he said was once a castle. We stood outside the iron gates, which were open but guarded by Polish police. My father told us that the castle was once owned by a noble family, but was taken over during the Austrian occupation and then used as a county courthouse and prison. When they were still living in Tyczyn, my grandfather Henry was arrested by the Gestapo and kept in this prison for more than six months. My father stood frozen, not wanting to go through the gates. "Come on," I said. "We're going in." I was tired of walking around Poland feeling unwelcome and afraid. They may have chased my father from this town, I told myself, but this time we had come back to find answers and I wouldn't turn back without them.

The police let us pass without even a glance, and as we approached the building my father moved towards a small plaque mounted near the doors. He read the words: "In memory of the 4,000 victims of Hitlerian terror who were held here, tortured, and murdered from 1939 to 1944." Then he added in his own words: "Among them was my father, your grandfather." Here on the wall, engraved on the shiny brass plaque and secured in history was the declaration of what had happened to my grandfather Henry Salzman.

We had returned to Rzeszów, a significant part of my father's upbringing that became a place of great suffering in the ghetto. Perhaps it was foolish of me, in this town where my father had lost his parents, to expect to find the closure with my father that the Holocaust had made impossible.

TYCZYN

As we moved deeper into Poland, the emotional weight of the things we had seen grew heavier—especially for me, sitting in the middle row of the van, listening to a CD of sad Hasidic melodies. Our current drive was from Rzeszów to Tyczyn, the town where my father grew up, but about which he was mostly silent. I knew that the worst was yet to come—that my father would have to reveal his most carefully guarded memories at last. The scenic views of the countryside couldn't erase the knowledge of the terrible things that had taken place in these pretty little towns.

If I felt overwhelmed by the trauma of the Holocaust, I could not even guess how my father was handling it; he appeared to be in a state of intractable grief. He seemed to become more nervous and emotional as Tyczyn approached. Finally, we passed the sign signaling our entry into Tyczyn. I felt my eyes well up with tears. My father had come home.

The streets began to narrow, and old, dilapidated wooden houses appeared among the trees. My father started calling out the places he recognized. I tried to take in and memorize every passing site. There was the pond where he used to go ice skating during the winter with his brother, Manek. There was the Old Town drugstore. My father began to laugh when he recognized the house where he had taken his one and only piano lesson. There was so much he had forgotten but it was all coming back now. He told the driver to turn left down a small side alley. My father pointed out the cemetery on the right and the house where the rabbi lived on the left. There was the gray, one-story building that was the house of charity for the poor people in Tyczyn. My father asked the driver to park so we could get out and walk.

We first walked to the Rynek, the town square. The square was just a small green space bordered by streets with old houses and a smattering of shops. In a way, my father seemed surprised that any of these places still existed and that his past had not been completely erased. He led us around the square and pointed out all the places that were a part of his childhood. First was the little yellow house that belonged to the Tuchmans, one of the many Jewish families he knew; then another small building where his parents' friends, the Goldmans, once had a business. We passed the post office and the doctor's house. My father pointed out a narrow street where the Tyczyn Synagogue once stood. He told us how the Nazis burned the prayer books and the Torah scrolls in the street.

We tried to talk to anyone we could find on the road. But few people were out on this sunlit morning, and those who were out walking seemed uninterested in us. Among those who were, no one had heard of my father's family or of any other Jews who had returned since the war. Several people exclaimed that we were the first Jews to come back at all. It was a ghost town for Jews.

Looking down a steep hill, my father pointed out a small red building where he had worked as the apprentice to a locksmith during the Nazi occupation but before going to the Rzeszów ghetto. He told us how the locksmith gave him a few potatoes to share with his family.

The fragments of stories and places we had heard about were coming to life. We walked to his old elementary school, and as we stood outside, my father told us how he was sent home on the first day that the schools opened after the Germans came into Tyczyn and forbade Jewish students to attend school. The sides of the old building were made of logs, the cracks between them filled with moss and clay. We passed another small, crumbling house and he told us that this was where one of the Jewish refugee families from Kalish lived. The family had three daughters, and the middle girl, Ruth, was his brother's girlfriend.

An old woman with white hair was walking down the street towards us. As she came closer, my mother called out to her in Polish. She stopped and spoke with my parents in Polish for a few moments and then turned in the direction that we were heading and began to walk with us. She was speaking with great excitement, and I could make out the names of several families I had heard my father mention. We turned down another street and began to walk down a steep hill. My father was still speaking to the woman in Polish. Suddenly, he stopped and looked at an old house at the bottom of the hill. "It's my house," he said. "It's my house."

A large, old white house with a crimson metal roof stood on the small corner lot. The yard was overrun with weeds. The lowest level of the three-story house was built of stone and the upper floors of stucco. The house appeared to be under renovation. More stones were piled up in the yard along with workmen's supplies. My father had told us before we arrived in Tyczyn that if we came to his house and it was still standing, he would not want to go in or even knock on the door. But in this woman's company, with her excitement at our unexpected return, he simply followed her as she made her way up the winding front walk to the front door and rang the bell. We stood together with great anticipation in front of the heavy wooden door to my father's house.

An old man answered the door. He knew the woman we had met on the street. She spoke to him in Polish and then turned and introduced my father to him. My father told the man his American name and then the name he had before the war and the names of his parents. The man shook my father's hand and seemed happy to meet the former resident of his house, although he denied knowing my grandparents. He invited us to come in to see what improvements and changes had been made.

We crowded into the small entry. The floor of the entry and the steps up the wide staircase to the main floor landing were laid with an intricate pattern of brown and tan tiles. My father began to climb the stairs. "This is how it was," he kept repeating. "This is how it was." The man who now owned the house led us up to the main level, showing us how he had made the rooms over into individual boarding rooms for rent. The walls and ceiling along the hallways were badly in need of repair. Clothes and laundry had been strung along the staircase railing.

We passed the kitchen, my grandmother's kitchen. A faded red paisley curtain separated the kitchen from the hallway. A very old glass lamp hung from the ceiling. I wondered if the lamp was there when my grandmother lived here. I was standing in the heart of the house, where my grandmother cooked and served meals to her family. This was the kitchen that my father's family had pushed their beds into and slept in during the winters of the Nazi occupation when there was only enough coal to heat one room in the house. This was the kitchen where my grandparents had spent long, desperate hours meeting with their Jewish neighbors and friends as they tried to figure out how to cope with the worsening demands and conditions imposed by the Nazis. This was the kitchen where my grandmother had sat and despaired for more than six months after my grandfather was arrested by the Gestapo and taken away. I looked at the broken and dirty tile floor and the kitchen sink, which was filled with dishes. This was as close as I could get to her.

We walked up another flight of stairs and came to my father's old bedroom. The small and cluttered room had an old shabby sofa pushed up against the wall. Storage boxes, furniture, lamps, and other belongings were stacked up across the floor. My father pointed to one side of the room where his bed used to be and then pointed to another wall where he kept his desk. I remembered the stories he had told us of how he went to his room when it was time to move to the ghetto, and how he spent hours looking through his belongings in order to make the difficult and ultimately futile decision about what to take and what to leave behind.

He shook his head sadly, took one last look around the room, and led us back out into the hallway. "It's my house," he said. "But nothing is the same."

We followed the current owner through a maze of rooms and out onto a small balcony, where he proudly pointed out the view of Tyczyn, as if my father had not stood in this very place a lifetime ago. I pulled my brother Alan aside. "Come on," I said. "Let's go find the attic." It had been my dream to go into the attic of my grandparents' house. Maybe I would find something that belonged to my grandparents that I could give to my father— perhaps a small envelope of photos or letters hidden behind a beam. Maybe we would find my grandfather's carefully hidden prayer shawl. This was my chance and I was going to take it.

We went to the top floor. There were no attic openings in the ceilings like in our homes in America, but we saw a door down the hallway that looked unlike the others. It was made of rough wood and had a beaten-up old doorknob. The door was unlocked, so we opened it and stepped into the attic, a small room with an unfinished wood floor. Rows of metal bookcases had been set up along the walls and down the center of the room. We began looking through the books and boxes on the shelves. My brother told me right away that the books weren't old enough to have been from before the war. The boxes were full of supplies for the workmen's renovations. "There's nothing here," said my brother. I took a final look up to the rafters and could not accept that there was nothing left. I followed him out and closed the door behind us and returned downstairs to find our parents and brother.

We had found nothing and that was a tremendous disappointment. I tried to console myself with the fact that I had been to my grandparents' attic, and that I had searched. Though my hands were empty, my heart was filled with longing for the grandparents I never knew. And with those powerful feelings came the knowledge that they would always be my grandparents, even if they died before I was born. I realized as I stood in their home that they could and must love us, even from beyond, and that I could claim them. Through my brothers and me, the Salzman family would carry on. Across the great abyss created by the Holocaust, I had touched the traces of my father and my grandmother, Anna, whose name I carried. I had found something after all.

TOMASZÓW LUBELSKI

We left Tyczyn and drove the short distance to my mother's hometown, Tomaszów Lubelski. My mother, whose name was Ruth Nikelsberg until she married my father, had told me only a handful of stories about her parents, siblings, and grandparents. She had loving memories of the Sabbaths and holidays they spent together before the Nazis came. My mother worried that we should not be scarred by the stories of the Holocaust. I learned more about her experiences from a tape she made for the US Holocaust Memorial Museum and from the few conversations we had when I was older and had children of my own.

My mother was the oldest child in her family. She had two younger sisters, Fay and Sally, and a younger brother named Sol. They lived in Tomaszów Lubelski, a small town where nearly half the population was Jewish. Most of the Jews there, including my mother's family, were of modest means, and life for them was a constant struggle. The whole family lived in a two-room apartment. My grandfather did some kind of work involving lumber while my grandmother stayed at home with the children. In the summer of 1939, my mother went to visit an aunt in Warsaw, and that's where she was when the Germans invaded Poland on September 1, 1939. Each night during the German invasion, my mother and her aunt would climb down into the basement and huddle together while they waited for the bombings to end.

When the Germans occupied Warsaw, life became increasingly difficult and dangerous for the Jews. There were beatings, arrests, and growing restrictions by the Nazis. In the late fall of 1939, my mother's aunt put my mother, then about thirteen, on a train by herself to return to her family in Tomaszów. After only a few hours the train was stopped. German soldiers boarded the train and demanded that all the Jews get off. My mother stood among the crowd of Jews and onlookers. A tall Polish railroad worker came over to her, wordlessly took her hand, and tugged at her to walk away with him. She did. They walked down the road almost a mile to a cluster of run-down apartment buildings. He led her into a crowded apartment, where nearly twenty other Jews, adults and children, were being hidden. Some had been there a few days; others had been hiding there much longer. There was little space to try to sleep and barely any food, but at least they were safe from the roaming Nazis. This Christian stranger saved my mother's life.

My mother remained in the apartment for more than a month. One day, a different Polish worker came and told her it was time for her to leave and go back to her town. He walked her through deserted back roads and an overgrown field and gave her a small amount of money she could use to bribe peasants for food or help. She set off alone towards Tomaszów. For days, she walked and slept in the fields and was sometimes lucky enough to beg rides on the wagons of peasants and farmers heading east.

Finally, she made it to her town and her street. But a neighbor who knew her mother told her that all the Jews, including her family, were gone.

My mother had an aunt who lived in the nearby town of Komarów. Being young and blonde, my mother decided to take her chances and set out alone to find her aunt's home. Again, she walked and took rides when she could until she got to Komarów and found her aunt's small house. She knocked, and when Poles she didn't recognize answered the door, she stammered as she apologized for coming to the wrong house. Once again, she was too late. All the Jews of Komarów had disappeared. She didn't know where else to go, so she again returned to Tomaszów.

Her grandmother had started a small dairy delivery business in town. My mother remembered a kind man, a supervisor at a local hospital, who was on the delivery route. She went to the hospital and found him. She told him of her desperate search for her family and that she had nowhere else to turn. He somehow arranged to put her in a hospital bed and told her to pretend that she was a sick patient. Over the next few days, he quietly made inquiries and learned that her family had crossed the border and reached the Russian occupied town of Rawa-Ruska. After more than a week in the hospital, my mother was surprised and overjoyed when, very late one night, her own mother came into the hospital room. With the help of the Polish supervisor, they left the hospital safely; they bribed peasants and farmers to guide them through the fields and forests until they arrived safely in Rawa-Ruska. She was finally reunited with her family.

A few weeks later, there came a knock at the door, and a group of Russian soldiers ordered them out into the streets and onto waiting trucks. The Jews still in Rawa-Ruska were driven to the railroad station and loaded onto boxcars. They ended up traveling more than a month into the depths of Siberia. There they would spend the next two years living in primitive conditions and surviving the freezing and treacherous winters. They had little food to eat and were housed in crude barracks they had been forced to construct in the dense forest, out in the middle of nowhere.

When the war ended, they were allowed to cross the border back into Poland. They met survivors of the concentration camps: thin, haggard young men and women, many still in striped concentration camp uniforms, who told them of the terrible death and destruction that had taken the lives of millions of Jews across Europe.

Poland was in ruins and had become a giant graveyard. Except for the Jews who fled to the Russian zone, the Jews of Tomaszów Lubelski had been forced to walk the short distance to the Belzec extermination camp. The survivors warned my mother's family not to return to their homes or try to recover any of their belongings. The Poles were still killing Jews.

For the next few years, my mother was active in Poland and Germany in the underground Bricha (Escape) Movement, which was organized to help Jewish Holocaust survivors leave post-war-ravaged Europe. My mother worked with other Jews to find and collect the Jewish orphans who had survived the

Holocaust. Some were with Christian families who had been promised money to keep the children until the parents could return for them, but the parents had all been murdered. My mother helped find these orphans so they could be smuggled to Israel and live a Jewish life. Sometimes the Bricha members would pay off the families to get the Jewish children back. But sometimes the Polish farmers wanted to keep the children to work on their farms or in their homes, and my mother and fellow workers would have to snatch the children in daring and dangerous rescue attempts. Later, she traveled to Germany to escort and smuggle surviving Jews across borders and mountains on the journey to Israel.

Eventually, my mother herself traveled on a ship to Israel. After a while, she came to the United States to visit relatives in New York, and while she was there she met my father. At the time, he was an American soldier but also a survivor like her. They fell in love and my mother decided to stay in America.

We parked our van and started to walk through Tomaszów. As in other towns, our American clothes and the cameras around our necks drew stares. We walked the streets looking for signs and plaques that recorded the atrocities that had taken place here. We had begun to look at the doorposts of homes for the marks that revealed where a mezuzah had once been affixed and where a Jewish family had lived. The city was much larger than my father's town and was crowded with cars and people. We wandered the streets for a while, but my mother could not find her house. Nothing looked familiar. She was becoming upset, for she had very much hoped to find something from her past. She stopped a few elderly people and spoke with them, but they claimed to know nothing about the Jews who lived there before the war.

The two synagogues had been destroyed by the Germans. The cemetery had been demolished and the tombstones used to pave the roads in the town. We came to a busy corner and my mother pointed to a large brick building. "That was the fire-house," she said. "It has been rebuilt." She told us how the Germans took hundreds of Jews from the town, locked them in, and then set the building on fire. She remembered how the flames came out the windows and the roof was ablaze. She remembered the screams of the people being burned alive.

We walked down another street and came to an old church. "I remember this church," she said. "I remember how afraid I was to even walk past it. Once the Germans came, our neighbors and friends became our enemies. We Jews were no longer welcome or safe in our own town or even in our homes. We had nowhere to go and no one in our town we could turn to." I linked my arm through my mother's as we walked down the cobblestone street. Softly I began to sing in Hebrew, "Am Yisrael Chai: The People Israel Live." My mother began to sing with me and our voices grew louder. I turned to her and assured her that no one on the streets of Tomaszów Lubelski would recognize the language we were singing in. "They didn't win," I told my mother. "Our faith and our people live on."

BELZEC

We had driven hundreds of miles across Poland. I had seen and felt so much that I was exhausted and numb. I fell asleep quickly each night, and tossed and turned as my mind wrestled with the intense and emotional experiences that filled each day. My heart was heavy and my eyes were tired from crying. It seemed as though we couldn't go a mile in any direction without a marker that identified a site of the Holocaust.

We were driving to Belzec. That morning's silence was full and heavy from our dark despair. This is the place I had dreaded visiting but also the place that had drawn me to Poland. We had been to many ghettos and concentration camps, but no place seemed as foreboding. Belzec is the name of both the town and the Nazi extermination camp where 600,000 Jews were murdered in the gas chambers in a mere eleven months. The camp was closed when no more Jews were left in the surrounding villages and cities. Among the victims were my paternal grandparents, Anna and Henry Salzman, and almost all the relatives from my father's family. While my mother and her immediate family escaped to the Russian zone, most of the Jews from Tomaszów Lubelski were unable to escape and were killed at Belzec.

We had come on a sacred mission. We were returning to Belzec to say Kaddish for my grandparents and other relatives, along with the hundreds of thousands of Jews with no one left to mourn for them. We would be standing where our ancestors stood, and where they had died in a sea of gas and flames, their cries unanswered.

For the first few miles of our drive, we filled the van with our idle chatter about the weather, our dinner the previous night at a lively Polish restaurant, and our recollections of other car trips we had taken as a family. We were making an effort to seem cheerful for my father's sake, but there was an unmistakable tension. My brothers were sitting in the last row of the van. My mother sat in the front and spoke to the driver in Polish, while I sat in the middle row next to my father. After a while, we turned off a busy highway and began driving along an empty and narrow road. The trees on both sides became taller and thicker, and soon it seemed that we were driving right into the forest. Our guide told us that, indeed, these pine forests were considered to be the thickest woods in Poland. I stared into them as we drove closer to Belzec, and as I watched the dancing pockets of light cast by the morning sun, my thoughts turned to the doomed Jews who had fled their homes and towns and tried to survive in these forests. How could any of them have hoped to survive without food, shelter, or help from the outside world? For a small number, the forests were their only chance for survival. I remembered my father telling us that, when the Nazis came at night to his town, his family would often run from their home and hide in the woods, sometimes waiting all night before they dared venture back to their residence.

I looked over at my father, who was staring silently out the window. I reached over and took his hand and felt the soft warm flesh of his palm. This was the same hand that had taken mine to help me cross the street when I was a little girl, and the hand that held my arm as he walked me down the aisle at my wedding. It was the hand that had carried me, guided me, and kept me safe my whole life. Now it was my turn to take his hand, to let him know without words that he was not alone.

Suddenly, out the window I saw train tracks. They ran along the road just a few yards inside the woods, and as we drove, they fell in and out of my view. This is it, I thought. This is the last road they traveled. We slowed as we passed on the left a small railway station with a green sign that said "Belzec." This is where the boxcars had unloaded my family. When I heard my father was crying, I knew that he must have seen it too.

We turned into a small gravel parking lot. There were no other cars in sight. We got out of the van and walked towards a large double metal gate that led into the camp. The gates had been left open just wide enough for us to pass through. The iron had been welded in sharp black spokes shaped like barbed wire, and in the middle were the dates "1942–1943."

We walked onto the grounds of Belzec and saw to our immediate right a few signs posted in an unkempt patch of weeds and grass. One of them displayed a large map of the camp, with a section of the legend at the bottom written in Polish and English. Among the locations listed and numbered were the guardhouses, the places for prisoners to undress and leave their clothes, the gas chambers, and the largest area, which held mass graves. As we went farther into the camp, I saw my mother lovingly place her arm around my father's waist as they walked together. I knew that her touch conveyed strength and love, and that she would support and guide my father through this field of death and destruction.

We came to a small monument in the middle of an empty field. There was a low platform with a metal sculpture representing two bent and emaciated humans. One seemed to be trying to hold up the other, who was bent over as if collapsing. Again, there was a scattering of memorial candles and withered flowers at the base of the memorial. It seemed as though Belzec was just a tiny forest with unmarked graves.

My father turned to us. "Okay," he said. "We've been here. Let's go back."

"Let's go farther," I said and began to walk on. We had been in Belzec for less than twenty minutes, and I was not ready to leave.

As we walked deeper into the camp, a man stepped out from among the trees. He was shirtless and smoking a cigarette. He approached us in a friendly manner and spoke in English with a British accent. He told us that he was working there as an inspector, overseeing the excavation of the camp as part of an international project to build a new memorial at Belzec. Then he took some folded maps out of his pocket and began telling us about that effort and what they had discovered at Belzec: more than thirty-two mass graves. He showed us on the maps the sites of the forester's cottage, the barracks, and several mass graves with more than 15,000 intact unburned corpses and six sacks of skulls.

We kept walking with him and he led us to the site where there had been a crematorium. He told us that the patches of sandy ground we now stood on were mixed with human ashes. We saw a crew of his workers digging deep holes to locate and mark the sites of the mass graves. They were pulling up samples of the dirt to see where the brown earth was mixed with the gray cremains. The inspector told us that, after a heavy rain, he often found large pieces of bone that he would give to the rabbi in Warsaw for a proper burial. He described the terrible smell back in October when it was freezing cold and they had found the graves, even though the bodies had been buried fifty-six years ago. He told us that, in his view, Belzec was one huge cemetery. When he first started working on the project, he was surprised that locals came to have picnics there; after the weekends he and his crew often found empty vodka bottles.

My father mentioned that his parents had been deported to Belzec from the Rzeszów ghetto during the first weeks of July 1942. The inspector then took us farther into the woods to a spot where the victims from Galicia, the region that included my grandparents' town, were buried in a mass grave.

He stopped us before a descending dirt path and told us that it led to the gas chambers, which had been built below ground. I looked down the short path. This was where my grandparents had taken their last steps.

We thanked him for the unofficial tour and walked by ourselves back to the memorial near the entrance to the camp. I took out several yahrzeit memorial candles. My rabbi in Texas had prepared copies of prayers for me to bring to Belzec and had even made a tape of the prayer "El Malei Rachamim," which asks God to grant peace to the souls of the departed.

In front of the memorial sculpture we tried to light the yahr-zeit candles, but the wind was gusting and the wicks wouldn't stay lit, though we tried to shield them with large stones and broken bricks. I gave my parents and brothers each a little sta-pled packet of prayers, and we began to recite the Mourner's Kaddish. As soon as we began, my mother started to cry. My father, brothers, and I went on with the prayer. I thought I would be the strong one, but I was the next to falter. I was crying too hard to recite the words that I had so painstakingly prepared. I heard my oldest brother Henry's voice break as he began to cry, and then my father's weeping. Only my brother Alan was left saying the prayer. In that moment I realized that we had to hold each other up, that none of us could do this alone. I began to pray out loud again, and then my father and Henry joined in, our prayers and our cries mixing together.

We finished our Hebrew prayers. The rabbi had suggested that I ask everyone in the family to take a moment and speak in our own words from our hearts. I had not thought I could find anything to say worthy of the importance of our family memo-rial service. It seemed safer to rely on the traditional prayers and rituals. But then the moment came to leave, and I knew that none of us were finished. My mother couldn't stop crying. My parents held each other and they started to walk towards the gate, but I called them back.

My brothers and I took turns speaking. We testified to the honorable and courageous lives our parents had led. We spoke of how much we longed for the grandparents we never knew and how proud they would have been to see how my father had grown up and what a mensch he had become, fulfilling their final wish to him. He had not wasted the gift of life he was given. He had come out from the Holocaust, a broken shell of a man, and lived up to every ideal and dream that his beloved parents might have hoped for. He had a wife and children whom he loved and who loved him in return. He had kept his faith in God and passed on the Jewish faith that they had died for. This was all we could do: to offer up our love and our lives as a way to honor and keep their memories alive. We vowed never to forget them.

My father stood like a broken man, alone in his grief and pain. "I'm here, Dad," I said. "You're not alone, and you will never be alone again."

I left Belzec that day, but a part of me remained there—a part of my heart that broke and fell with tears onto that burial ground. And a part of Belzec remains with me. I will never again see a train track without remembering. I will never think of my beloved grandparents without remembering that I stood on the path they stumbled down on their way to the gas chambers.

PART THREE

Interconnections

MAKING ADJUSTMENTS

On the morning of my return to the United States, I changed my Lufthansa flight with a layover in Frankfurt to a nonstop from Warsaw to Dallas. I felt completely drained and just wanted to get back to my husband, my children, and my life. I couldn't wait to sleep in my own bed and wake up without dread. I longed for a day without tears. I needed to return to the world of the living and put the past aside for a while. As I made my way through customs and saw my husband and children waiting for me, I could not hold back my tears.

My friends were calling and asking about the trip. It had been both wonderful and terrible, but I couldn't find the words to explain how this trip had changed my life. One of the best things about it was that I had grown closer to my brothers and parents. We had brought each other comfort and strength and learned to open our hearts to one another.

People repeatedly asked me if we had found closure. That was not why I undertook the journey; I went to excavate our past and locate a truer sense of myself. When I had my photos developed, I spread them out on the bed and looked over what I had captured: a collage of train tracks and concentration camps, of barren synagogues and ovens overflowing with ashes, of surprised faces of the people who lived in my grandparents' house and didn't care that their riches came from my family's ruins.

I resumed my daily activities: took my kids to play dates, stopped at the store to pick up groceries for dinner, chatted with the clerk at the dry cleaner, and waved to a neighbor in the morning as I went out to pick up the newspaper. I fought the constant pull to turn inward and relive the trip to Poland. I swallowed and pushed down the grief that I knew one day would surface. The despair I felt as I stood at the ash pits of Auschwitz and at the empty fields in the Płaszów camp, in my mother's town and my father's house, reemerged in the tears that collected in the corners of my eyes.

I cried when I was in the shower and when I drove alone in the car. I went for walks and listened to the same sad Jewish music I had listened to in Poland and hid my eyes behind sunglasses. In my waking and sleeping hours, I could feel my father's hand in mine as we drove along the train tracks towards Belzec. I clung to the memory of those moments when I stood with my parents and brothers and, in our shared grief, our hearts connected and our pain was carried by the deep and strong love we had for each other. Now I was back in Texas, left to myself to sort and sift through the new pages in my family's history. I felt like I had as a child: alone with the Holocaust.

I called my dear friend Keith Stern, who had been my rabbi and teacher and was also a child of survivors. He had left Texas and relocated with his family to the Boston suburbs. We shared that special bond that exists between children of survivors;

though we both lived with two feet in this world, a part of our heart was in the world of our parents. Many years ago, he had led the consecration service at our synagogue for the Hebrew school grade that included his son and my daughter. As the group of young children stood on the bimah, their faces shining while they sang the Hatikvah, Israel's national anthem, I noticed that his eyes were brimming with tears. "They weren't supposed to be here," he said to me afterwards. "The Nazis tried to kill all the Jews, but thank God our parents survived and now we live to see this day." What a beautiful, awesome sight, this new generation of children.

The weight of our parents' past rested on our shoulders, and I dreaded passing it on to our own children. I finally understood why many survivors found it impossible to speak to their young ones about the atrocities of the Holocaust.

When I called Keith, he knew in an instant that I had changed. It was a mitzvah, he told me, a good deed, to go back with my parents, to walk with them through the ashes and through their grief. It was a mitzvah to try to console them, but he also knew that it had come at a terrible and permanent price. He told me that it was impossible to go to Auschwitz and not be changed. "Give yourself time," he told me. Deep down I was afraid that I would never be the same again, that sadness would continue to permeate my existence—that I had become like my father.

I confided to Keith that, since my return, I could no longer recite the Shema, Judaism's most important prayer affirming our belief in God, without crying. The prayer held a new power over me. I had stood in the forests, ghettos, and gas chambers where my people had, in their last moments, as Jewish custom decrees, cried out the Shema. I believed that my grandparents, suffocated in the poisonous gas chambers at Belzec, had called out to God with this prayer. Now, each time I said the Shema, I heard the echo of the past and remembered all those who had been tortured and who died while affirming their faith in God—a God who must have despaired from the heavens for the suffering of his people.

Yet I found a new strength and commitment to explore and reveal my Jewish identity. As I was living and raising my children in the Bible Belt, I often resorted to the same strategies my father had relied upon to survive in the ghetto and in the camps. He learned to live "in the middle." When the prisoners were marched through the camp, they were marched in formations of fives. My father learned to find his way to the middle. In the middle, he was less likely to be hit or pulled out by the brutal guards. In the soup lines, being in the front meant you risked getting the watery broth from the top of the soup barrel; if you ended at the back of the line, you risked that the meager soup would already be gone. Being in the middle was the way to stay alive. Look down, don't make eye contact, try not to be noticed. This was the way to avoid danger.

During my entire life, I had never worn a Star of David. Now I was living in a small town in Texas where crucifix pendants were as commonplace as wedding bands, and public Christian prayer was a normal part of every city council and school board meeting. Though there was no overt antisemitism, subtle discrimination pervaded the community, and Jews felt like outsiders. Many of the local residents were zealots in trying to push their faith upon me. They were concerned about saving my soul in the hereafter, and not about how they offended me in the here and now.

However, I could no longer live in the middle. I went into a neighborhood jewelry store and asked if they had any necklaces with the Jewish Star of David. They had none and couldn't remember ever having sold one. They offered to order a charm version from a catalog and sell me a chain to wear it on. In a few days, they called to say that the Magen David had arrived. I went to pick up the necklace and put it on in the parking lot. I would live openly, and even defiantly, as a Jew.

I began to wear the delicate Jewish star outside my clothes. I didn't care anymore if people knew I was Jewish. I had friends who wouldn't put a mezuzah on their door because their neighbors would then treat them differently. I only wished that I had purchased the necklace sooner and had worn it in Poland. I was disappointed in myself and in the world for making it so hard to be me, so hard to be Jewish. Too many people had died so that I could live as a Jew. I was determined to live with the same courage that my ancestors had shown. The necklace became for me a symbol of the chain that links generations. "Am Yisrael Chai," through me also, "The People Israel Live."

I made the difficult decision to leave my synagogue and, with a few other Jewish families, formed a new congregation. Though I felt at home in my old synagogue, which was nearly twenty miles away, I wanted to feel at home in my own community. I had been to Poland, a place with many synagogues and no Jews. Now I was in a place with Jews and no synagogue. It was a *shanda*, the Yiddish word for a shameful thing.

If we could sing Hebrew on the streets of Poland, then we were more than ready for Texas.

THE 23RD PSALM

Right after the argument I had with my father, he started writing down the story of his life. This task intensified after our trip to Poland. He had been planning to retire from his aerospace career and move with my mother to sunny South Florida. Between the years in upstate New York and Maryland, they had endured enough winters and wanted to live in a place without cold weather and snow.

Writing gave my father a new goal and distracted him from his worries about retirement and moving to a new place. He set up an old card table and a folding chair in the basement of the Maryland house and bought a computer. Each night he wrote down every incident and detail he could remember. I was living in Texas and never read the work while it was in progress. My mother said that she was keeping after him to write. By the time they were packing up their furniture and moving to Florida, my father had filled over six hundred pages.

Once they had settled into their new home amid the palm trees and sun-tanned golfers, my father sent the complete manuscript with an aggressive cover letter to agents and publishers around the country. While some responses showed tentative interest, many of the agents and publishers failed to even send back a generic "No thank you" form letter. My mother called me every time a disappointing letter came or another week went by without any response to tell me how discouraged my father was becoming. I worried that he would think it was his life that was being judged unworthy among a sea of "how to" books, memoirs of the rich and famous, and other titles, not realizing that it might have more to do with timing or with the publisher's commercial criteria. My mother asked me, an amateur writer, to look over the manuscript and suggest some changes or ideas to help improve his publication prospects.

My father packaged up a printed copy of the manuscript and sent it to me in a brown box. The day it came I sat at my kitchen table with the manuscript before me. I had waited a lifetime for answers about his past, and here was a mountain of pages filled with names, dates, places, and accounts of the atrocities he had witnessed and survived.

I began to weave my way through my father's heartbreaking story. My father, his parents, and his entire family came alive in those pages. Their suffering, their courage, and their resilience brought me closer to them than ever before. Their words and deeds, recorded by my father, made me long for them and mourn their lost lives.

The manuscript carried me back in time: I stood in the garden behind my father's house; I was by my grandmother's side in her kitchen while she prepared soup from their dwindling rations for my grandfather, who became gravely ill after he was arrested, jailed, and beaten by the Gestapo; I was with my father when he was sent home from school after the Nazis' occupation, when he was beaten up by a German soldier, when he decided to protect his parents by not telling them, and during all the events he related. He was forced to jump up and down and crouch before the Nazi soldiers during the selection in the ghetto. That was when he watched families being forced apart and saw that those who tried to protect their parents, spouses, or children were shot at close range—and when he said goodbye to his parents forever before they were sent to their death in the gas chambers at Belzec.

My father wrote about the ten concentration camps he was sent to in Poland, Germany, and France, where he worked in the salt mines, dug up graves, carted dead bodies to the crematorium, and cleared rubble in the snow with only rags covering his feet. He described the barracks and the boxcars, the bitter cold winters and the near-starvation. He almost lost all hope and strength; he was preparing to die.

Some friends shared their last rations with him and helped him to the soup lines when he was too weak to walk on his own. Most of them died, leaving my father the responsibility to remember and speak for them. Finally, on May 2, 1945, a handful of American soldiers in olive uniforms cut through the barbed wire fence of the Wöbbelin concentration camp and liberated him before he, too, was added to the piles of dead bodies all around him.

I inserted the disk of the manuscript into my computer and began, delicately and apprehensively, to edit the giant work. I took out the extra spaces between the lines and narrowed the too-wide margins. I removed any references to what was going on around the globe as the war progressed that my father could not have possibly known at the time. I excised sentences that looked into the future, and the ones some fifty years later that looked back. He was back in captivity when he was telling his story, and that's where readers needed to be so we could see through his eyes.

From Texas I called my father every day and reread the manuscript with him, paragraph by paragraph, line by line. Our conversations elicited new memories of people he had known and things that had happened. I wrote as he spoke. I asked him to fill in his descriptions of people, such as my grandmother, so that I could see her and feel her presence. I asked him about the long and terrible nights in the camps, about what it was like to spend three years all alone in that hell.

I cried each day as I worked on his memoir. I also wondered why I had been allowed to be a part of this important work. I was moved by the stories of the Christian strangers who saved his life, time and time again, with acts of kindness. There was the extra bowl of soup that he received for a few days when his job was to clean the barrel the soup was served in. He in turn shared the soup with his friends, who were also starving. There was the German factory supervisor who arranged for him an easier job in the camp for a few weeks while my father was recovering from a knee injury and infection. The German supervisor pulled him off a truck filled with weak and ill prisoners being taken away to be killed.

I recited the words of his story until I knew nearly every word by heart. For hours each day I disappeared into his past as I worked on the book, and then I had to transform myself back into the cheerful, functional mom who would cook dinner and take her kids to soccer games. I weighed and worried about each word that I changed and prayed that my work would help ease my father's sorrow and help him heal.

In the midst of this, my father was diagnosed with cancer. I flew my parents to Texas, where he underwent surgery and a two-week hospital stay. It was a few days before Thanksgiving. My brothers and I joined forces to help our parents through the hospitalization and difficult recovery. The trip to Poland had changed our relationship with my father. He no longer hid his emotions. Now he needed his wife and children to support him, and he let us see his fear. In the hospital, as he was about to be taken to surgery, the nurse asked us to say good-bye. I leaned over and asked my father if he wanted me to go with him. He nodded his head yes. I took his hand and walked along as he was being wheeled to the operating room, and I stayed with him in pre-op until he was asleep. He had never been a patient in a hospital. He had to let go and trust that his doctors and his family would care for him and that we would be by his side when he woke. I would be strong for my father.

After his surgery, my parents stayed with me in Texas for several weeks. It was hard for my father to accept his illness. After a few days a male nurse came to our house to check his vital signs.

When the nurse was about to leave, I said, "Tell him something. He's so unhappy. Can't you tell him something to give him hope?"

The nurse walked around the table to my father and said, "Stand up. I'll show you something I learned in Vietnam." He gently put his arms around my father's shoulders and held him. "Here's the secret," he said. "You can't do it alone. You must let other people help you. And when you're better, then you go and help someone else."

It wasn't a secret. It was the same wisdom that had helped my father survive the Holocaust.

My father returned to Florida, and after a few months the work on the book was complete. We submitted it to a well-respected university publisher and waited to hear from them. After a few weeks, I received a call that they would consider the manuscript, but that it would have to go through a review process that would take several months. We were prepared to wait it out, and if it was not accepted we would go on to find another publisher. The book was sent to two outside readers, both considered to be experts in the field of Holocaust studies. They were to respond with their candid remarks and opinions on whether the book should be published.

One afternoon, after my kids had just climbed in the car and we were heading out to run errands and grab lunch, the mail truck stopped in front of the house. I pulled up next to the mailbox and grabbed the handful of letters. At a stoplight I glanced through the pile and saw a letter from the University of Wisconsin Press. I was afraid to open it. We went to eat and I quickly settled my kids at a table while I opened the letter. After reading the first few sentences, I began to cry. A professor at Boston College had written a wonderful and supportive review. He had been touched and changed by my father's story.

I dialed my parents on my cell phone. My father picked up and my mother listened in. I read the review to them. It was liberation all over again—the liberation of his painful story that he alone had carried. At first there was only silence from their end of the phone, and then I could hear that they were both crying. We had not been wrong. The story of what happened to my father mattered. The second review was just as positive. A few weeks later, we received a contract for the book.

My parents came to Texas in the fall for the Jewish holiday of Rosh Hashanah, the New Year. We had just returned from a luncheon held after the morning service. As we pulled into the driveway, I saw a brown box, which contained the published copies of his book, *The 23rd Psalm: A Holocaust Memoir*. I handed a copy to my father, who held it gently in his hands and turned the pages, marveling that he was holding his own book. On the original cover was a blend of two photographs of my father. The one on the bottom was from a picture taken of him and three friends by an American soldier on the day they were liberated from the Wöbbelin concentration camp. Pictured are the legs of the four gaunt young men, who are leaning on each other as they walk through the camp. They are dressed in the ragged, striped uniforms worn by the prisoners. The top picture was a close-up of my father, taken a few months after he was liberated. He was then living in one of the many displaced persons camps, where he would remain for two years until he was able to come to America. His thick black hair had just begun to grow back, and he was, after three years as a prisoner in the camps, wearing civilian clothes. His eyes, dark and serious, stare out from the photo. They are not the eyes of a seventeen-year-old but the sad and knowing eyes of an old man.

I held my father's book in my hands and knew that his heart and his spirit could now be lifted. Every person who would read his story and the stories of those he knew would carry some of those memories in their own hearts. It had been too much for my father to carry alone.

PARACHUTING IN

While my father and I were working on *The 23rd Psalm,* we were plagued with doubts and uncertainties. We wondered if anyone would want to read my father's story. We kept telling ourselves and each other that it really didn't matter if the book sold. My father was writing to fulfill his obligation to bear witness. He had testified for the sake of his children, grandchildren, and future generations. He had been the lone branch left in our family tree and we were the new forest that grew out of the wreckage.

However, the connections began even before the book was published. At first, I couldn't believe the coincidences when people turned up who were linked to my father's story. After they became more frequent, I began to believe that this was all meant to be, that my father's story had the stories of others within it.

The first connection had to do with the book itself. We were in the final stages of preparation before the book would go into print. While working in the Pentagon, my father had come across the cover photograph of himself with three other prisoners. It was in a pictorial history of the World War II 82nd Airborne, called *The Devils in Baggy Pants*, after the nickname given to the American parachutists by a German soldier who saw them descending from the skies. The book contained individual and group photographs of some of the soldiers in the 503rd and 504th infantry regiments and, in the last few pages, some photographs taken during the liberation of the Wöbbelin concentration camp. Among the images was the photograph of my father and the three other prisoners, who had become his friends in the camp. They walked, leaning on each other, all wearing the striped concentration camp uniforms. The Pentagon librarian found a second damaged copy of the *The Devils in Baggy Pants*, which he gave to my father. This small act of kindness would have to wait forty years before it would reveal an important and powerful connection.

We sent the book to the University of Wisconsin Press permissions editor, Margaret Walsh, to see if the photo could be included in my father's memoir. Margaret, while looking through the book, found a photo of her own father, William Walsh, who served in the 82nd Airborne and was one of the handful of American soldiers who opened the gates of the camp and liberated my father.

In my efforts to publicize the book, I sent an email to CNN telling of this unexpected and wonderful connection. Within a few hours, I received a reply that CNN would like to accompany me and my father to Wisconsin to meet the Walsh family, including the widow of William Walsh.

At the University of Wisconsin Press offices we waited nervously in the lobby. The CNN crew wanted to film and interview the Walsh family before our meeting. I had arranged to have flowers brought in that I could give to William Walsh's widow. At last we were summoned to the conference room and greeted by a roomful of smiling faces. We exchanged hearty handshakes and a few hugs with the Walsh family. It felt more like a reunion than a first meeting.

It turned out that William Walsh had spoken little of his experiences to his children when they were younger. Each had heard bits and pieces of his war history, including the liberation of the Wöbbelin camp. He had spoken of the terrible stench he smelled for miles before he reached the camp and the surprise of finding emaciated prisoners lying among the dead bodies.

After that Walsh said nothing more about the war and the past. When he was finally ready to talk about it again, he suffered a stroke that left him unable to speak. He passed away in 1992 with much of his story untold.

We stood around the conference table looking at photos of William Walsh as a young, handsome soldier, and display cases filled with the many medals and ribbons he had been awarded, among them two Purple Hearts and the Distinguished Service Cross. My father embraced Mrs. Walsh and thanked her for her husband's great bravery. He then turned to the children and grandchildren gathered around the table. He expressed his sincere gratitude for the generation of young American soldiers, including their father, who had come to his rescue when all hope was lost.

We left the crowded conference room and went outside so the CNN crew could tape some of the family members individually. While we were standing in the parking lot, one of the

Walsh sons came over to me. He told me that his father had cut down and kept the flag that had hung over the camp. He had it right there, in the trunk of his car. Out of concern about how my father would react to seeing it, he had not brought it to the conference room. I asked my father if he wanted to see it. Without hesitation, he said he did. The son brought over a small plastic grocery bag and held it out to us. My father reached in and I helped him pull out and unfold a giant red flag with a large black swastika in the center. My father looked at the flag and shook his head with disgust. "I'm glad," he said, "that if it has to exist, it exists in a closet or attic and no longer hangs on a flag pole." "No," said one of the Walsh sons, "it will never hang again."

We went to lunch and celebrated and sealed the new connection between us. Their father had given my father his freedom, and my father had given them a new memory of their father as a hero. Similar events would happen again and again. My father's story was not just his own.

YOUR HUDDLED MASSES

Emil Ringel was one of my father's closest friends during the Holocaust. They met at the very beginning, after my father was separated from his parents and brother and taken to work and live in the Reichshof Labor Camp in Rzeszów, Poland, approximately ninety miles east of Kraków. My father was only fourteen and in desperate need of a friend. Emil and my father were put into the same barrack in the camp and assigned to the same work group. They quickly became close and trusted friends. This was critical, my father pointed out, for they were both younger than most of the prisoners and without families to look after them. To survive, one needed more than luck. "One needed a friend," said my father. "Someone who would watch your back and warn you of new and impending dangers, whom you could trust not to steal your shoes while you were sleeping."

I knew the Ringels from a distance when I was growing up. They lived in New York while we were in Maryland. I knew that Emil was a friend of my father's from that "before" time that we never spoke about. Emil, his wife, Clara, and children, Barbie and Jay, came to both of my brothers' Bar Mitzvahs. Though

Emil died of cancer when he was a young father, my parents kept a close friendship with Clara and her children. My father always spoke of Emil with great admiration and affection.

It wasn't until I read the draft of *The 23rd Psalm* that I began to understand the importance of Emil's relationship with my father. They stuck together and stayed alive through all ten concentration camps, the terrible travels in the boxcars, the endless and brutal roll calls, the heavy labor in the freezing winters, the long and lonely nights on the crowded wooden shelves in the barracks, the beatings, the hunger, and the selections. They were together when they each learned that their families had been taken to Belzec and murdered. And after all the years of suffering and misery, they shared their first moment of freedom.

Emil left for America and married Clara, another survivor. Later, my father came to the United States to live in New York with his Aunt Pauline and Uncle Julius, who had escaped with their children from Vienna before the war started. They helped him to begin a new life in America. No one else from my father's family had survived.

Having only completed the fifth grade, my father began his education anew in America. He attended night school to learn English, and day classes to learn how to repair radios. One of his early jobs was delivering buttons in New York City before he became a television installer. In 1950 he was drafted into the United States Army and served for three years. Later, he passed elementary and high school equivalency tests and used the GI Bill to attend college, earning bachelor's and master's degrees.

One night he ran into Emil in a movie theater in New York—their first meeting since the war ended. Emil and Clara introduced my father to my mother, and they were among the small group who attended my parents' wedding. Having met the love of his life, my father was ready to recover from the war years of heartbreak and loss.

After *The 23rd Psalm* was published, I traveled to New York City with my children to meet my parents for my father's first speaking and signing event, held at the Museum of Jewish Heritage. The event was held in a room with a wall of windows overlooking Ellis Island and the Statue of Liberty.

My father told of his struggles and survival. With the Statue of Liberty behind him, he recalled the first time he glimpsed it from the deck of the boat that brought him from Germany, and how wonderful it felt to see the magnificent symbol of American liberty.

Many of my mother's relatives and some of my friends who lived in New York and New Jersey came to see my father and hear him speak. Clara was there with her children. My father's cousin Erica, his Aunt Pauline's daughter, attended with her grown children, Ray, Monica, and Michael. Here in this room was the family of my father's dear friend and his only living relatives from before the war. They were my family.

Emil's children, Barbie and Jay, read my father's book. Their father had died before he told them much about what he had endured during the Holocaust. Barbie told me that her own father had come to life through my father's words. Emil's kindness and bravery, his loyalty and friendship, shone like a bright light from the dark years of suffering and despair.

A few months later, my parents flew to Washington, DC, to attend a weekend of events in honor of the ten-year anniversary of the United States Holocaust Memorial Museum. There were special tours of the museum and many speeches. A gathering of Holocaust survivors took place under large white tents on the lawns outside. Inside the tents were round tables, and each held a sign with the name of a ghetto, town, or camp. The survivors gathered at these tables, hoping to find someone from their hometowns or someone they may have crossed paths with during the war years. There was no table with a sign for my father's town of Tyczyn. Nevertheless, my resourceful father took a piece of cardboard, made his own sign, and sat at an empty table. No one came. Eventually, a curious reporter took his photograph, which later appeared in newspapers across America as a testimony to the resilience of hope against impossible odds.

After he returned to Florida, my father wrote an essay that was printed in *The Forward*, a Jewish newspaper in New York. He shared his views on the meaning of the gathering and the obligation of those who survived to speak and record what they had experienced. He mentioned the Margaret Walsh connection. He described his liberators and his fellow prisoners who did not live to tell their own children what they had endured. I contacted Barbie and told her about the article in *The Forward*, which mentioned her father.

The next day she called and said that she had brought a copy of *The Forward* to the office where she had worked for many years. She told me that, although her closest friends knew that her father was a Holocaust survivor, it was not something she shared with everyone she worked with. However, she did share the article with a coworker, David Simpson, who had been sitting in the cubicle next to her for over three years.

David read the article and couldn't believe it. His father, Ted Simpson, also served in the 82nd Airborne and liberated a concentration camp during World War II. He called his father and asked him the name of the camp he had liberated. It was the Wöbbelin camp. Barbie and David had shared casual conversations and work-related discussions, never once realizing that their fathers had also been next to each other six decades earlier when they stood across the barbed wire.

A PROVIDENTIAL CALL

Such coincidences seemed like more than luck; perhaps they were, as many people tried to persuade me, fate, designed by the hand of God. Just speaking with someone who had read the book often turned out to be an emotional experience. Readers inquired about my childhood experiences, my travel to Poland, and my work with my father on his memoir. They wanted to speak to the real me, the person I had spent my life hiding.

I traveled with my father on many book tours to keep him company and manage the logistics. I couldn't imagine him having dinner alone in some small hotel after a day spent talking and reliving his stories from the Holocaust. I cherished these trips together, listening to him speak to hundreds of people and then watching as dozens lined up, often crying, to meet him and share their own stories with him.

One April, in observance of Yom HaShoah, the annual Holocaust Remembrance Day, we traveled on a weekend to speaking engagements in Boston and Milwaukee. It was a wonderful weekend but exhausting. We parted at the Milwaukee airport, from whence my father flew back to Florida and I to Texas. I arrived on a Sunday night with just a few hours left in the day to unpack, run to the grocery store, and help my kids prepare for another week of school.

At the time, I was serving as the membership chair for my synagogue. I loved that volunteer position because it enabled me to meet the families new to our town who were considering joining the temple. I was spending several hours on the phone each week reassuring them that, though our Jewish community and synagogue were small, we would welcome them.

The morning after I returned from the trip with my father, I received one of these phone calls, from a woman named Miriam. In a foreign accent she told me that we had actually spoken a few months before, and that she had lived in Texas for many years but that her family had been going to another synagogue some twenty-five miles away.

I was sorry I had picked up the phone. I was tired and still had lots to do and didn't have the energy or enthusiasm to sound warm and welcoming. I spoke to her for a few moments and just about decided to take her number and get back to her in a day or two. However, I was curious about her accent and asked her where she was from.

Miriam told me she was from Germany. I asked her, in true child-of-Holocaust-survivors style, where her parents were from. She told me that her mother was from Germany and still lived there, along with her two brothers and a sister. Her father, who was no longer alive, had been from Poland.

I could hear that she had begun to cry. I apologized for upsetting her. She told me that this day, this Monday, was Yom

HaShoah and that her father was a Holocaust survivor. I told her that my parents were also survivors and that I had just returned from a trip with my father in observance of Holocaust Memorial Day. I mentioned my father's book and asked her what town in Poland her father had come from. She told me that he was from a small town that no one had ever heard of. I asked her again for the name of the town. It was Kalish. I told her that I knew of that town, that the people from Kalish had been sent to the same ghetto as the people from my father's town.

Then I asked her where her father had been during the war. She told me that he had been in many labor and concentration camps but didn't know all the names. He had been liberated by the Americans from a German camp in 1945. Her family name was Waks. I recognized the name from my father's memoir.

As she cried softly, I stood at the kitchen counter holding the phone in one hand and my father's book in the other. I found the name on page 106. It was spelled differently, but such variations often occur when foreign names are translated into English. I didn't tell her, but instead inquired if I could call her back.

I hung up the phone and called my father. I asked him about the Wachs whom he had written about in the book. He said that Yitzhak Wachs was his friend. They met in the first camp and were together, along with Emil Ringel, through all ten camps. They became separated after liberation, and my father later heard that Yitzhak had stayed in Germany and married a German woman. I told him about the phone call from a new community member whose father had been named Waks and was from Kalish. He doubted that it could be the same person.

I called Miriam again. Now I was crying. I asked her what her father's first name was. She told me it was Ignatz. Then I asked for his Jewish name, because his friends would have called him by his given name in the camps. It was Yitzhak.

I related the conversation I had with my father and gave her the name of the ghetto my father had been in along with the list of camps. Her father had kept a small notebook with the names of the places he had been in during the war, she said, but it was at her sister's home in Germany. She would call the next day and see what she could find out. Some of the names of the camps as well as the ghetto sounded familiar. Miriam mentioned that her father had been liberated on May 2, 1945—the same day that my father had been liberated.

A few days later she emailed that they had found the notebook with the list of camps and the ghetto her father had been in and could even provide affidavits confirming that Yitzhak Waks had been in the same ghetto as my father and in all ten of the same camps in the same order. She scanned in a photo of Yitzhak taken shortly after the war. I emailed it along with the other information to my father. He called me back after a few minutes. "It's him," he told me. "It's my friend Yitzhak."

I had received a random phone call from a stranger living in my small Texas community, and she turned out to be the daughter of one of my father's closest friends in the camps. Even stranger, Miriam and I realized that we had met before. Several months earlier, her sister had been visiting from Germany at the same time my parents had been visiting me from Florida. Miriam now asked me if I had taken them to a certain bakery for lunch. I told her that I had, and I remembered that, while we were waiting in line, my mother, as she always did when she overheard conversation in a foreign language, began to converse with two young German women who were in line in front of us. It was rare to hear German or any other European language being spoken in our town. Miriam told me that she was at the bakery that day and remembered talking to my mother and that my father was sitting at a nearby booth, holding a spot for my mother and me.

When I called my parents to see if they remembered the German woman, my father, with his uncanny memory, remembered the two women, one of them wearing a white dress. We met once and did not make a connection. Now we were being given a second chance to retrieve our shared legacy.

Miriam and I became friends. Our fathers had been like brothers and I felt a sisterly devotion to Miriam, just like I had for Barbie Ringel. Our sons, who were close in age and roughly the same age as our fathers when they met, also became friends. My father wrote a letter to Miriam about what a wonderful, selfless, and courageous friend Yitzhak had been to him during the terrible years in the camps. He wrote of how Yitzhak had helped him when he was too weak to stand in line for food, when he needed help just to walk and words of comfort to face another hopeless day. Miriam's father had never spoken to her about his experiences in the ghetto and the camps. When she read my father's story, she finally learned what her father had endured.

Miriam and her family came to my son Aaron's Bar Mitzvah, and I proudly introduced them to my brothers and relatives at a family dinner we held the evening before. That same weekend, Clara Ringel and her daughter, Barbie, were there.

Barbie, Miriam, and I, the three daughters, were together for a lively Sabbath nearly sixty years after our fathers had all been together in the camps.

A year later, my parents flew to Texas for the Bar Mitzvah of Miriam's son. My father was called to the bimah for an Aliyah, offering the blessings before the Bar Mitzvah child chants in Hebrew from the scroll containing the Hebrew scriptures. The rabbi spoke of how my father was there to stand in for Yitzhak. It was a profound and emotional service. "In the camps we never dreamed," said my father, "that we might survive and that one day our children and our children's children would live in freedom as Jews. It is a miracle that after so many years we have found each other."

This had to be more than luck or mere chance. Miriam had found a trace of her father's past, and I had found someone who could understand and share my feelings about my father's history. It felt like the heavens had opened just enough to let us find each other.

EPILOGUE

My journey began years ago with an argument I had with my father. Yet together we excavated his memories about people and places from his Holocaust years. Indeed, my father's family, many of his friends, and his life were destroyed, and out of his seeming singularity he had shouted, "I am Adam!"

During our family's expedition in Poland, my father was able to grieve and to honor his murdered relatives. After his story was published, friends and rescuers emerged from the rubble of his past. My father was not alone.

In addition to William Walsh, we met another soldier of the 82nd Airborne who had liberated my father. James Megellas was the most highly decorated veteran of that division, and he lived a mere ten minutes from my Texas home. My father became friends with him and they later traveled together to Germany to the site of the Wöbbelin camp.

I never gave up searching for information about my father's family and his only brother, Manek, whom he assumed had died during the Holocaust. I found in records at Yad Vashem a list of Jews from Tyczyn who survived the war, which included my father's brother. I discovered with enormous sadness that, though he had been liberated, he was killed by local Poles in 1946. My father took great solace in knowing that his brother had tasted freedom, if only for a short while.

My father passed away after a sudden illness in 2016. Keeping his story alive has given me a way to stay close to him even after his death. In his memoir, my father frequently mentions a small group of prisoners who were with him from the ghetto through the ten concentration camps until their day of liberation. Over the years, some children of these survivors have contacted me after finding their fathers' names in the book. I still search, with the aid of modern technology and the ongoing release of Nazi records, for other survivors who shared my father's Holocaust experience. In addition to Ringel and Wachs, I have connected with the sons and daughters of other fellow prisoners—Mola Tuchman, Moses Ziment, Tobias Nussen, Motek Hoffstetter, and Leon Horn. None of their fathers had told their Holocaust stories; through my father's book they recovered their lost family history, and we formed everlasting bonds of friendship. I even learned the fate of some prisoners who did not leave families behind, like Itzok Rypp, who died in a hospital near the displaced persons camp in Germany when he was only nineteen, and Moses Verständig, who died alone in Sweden.

In Poland, in every place I visited, every empty synagogue and ghetto, every camp and mass grave, every forest and village, the murdered innocent men, women, and children called out to be remembered. There is not a Sabbath that I do not recite prayers for them.

One afternoon, before I traveled to Poland, I was sitting outside on a gorgeous day reading the Bible. I came to a passage that helped me understand what I wanted and needed to do for my father. It was Exodus 23:5: "When you see the ass of your enemy lying under its burden and would refrain from raising it, you must nevertheless raise it with him." We are obligated, I read, to help an animal with a heavy burden on its back. What if it was not an animal? What if it was a man and the burden was not on his back but on his heart? And the more so if this man was not an enemy or a stranger but someone I loved, like my father. I knew in that moment that I had to reach out to my father and help him bear the pain that lay upon his heart.

In the beginning, my mother and one of my brothers asked me to leave my father alone. They didn't want me to ask the questions, to unleash painful memories that he had buried. They feared for him. Other survivors who spoke and wrote about their time in the camps had killed themselves. But I persisted with my questions. And I was lucky and blessed that my father possessed the courage and strength to tell us his story. Once he did, we loved him even more for it.

After we began to ask questions, my father humbled us with the compassion he showed us as we heard about the terrible things he had seen. We learned that he had his own questions. He once asked me during a spirited discussion about faith and God, why God had not answered his prayers and let his parents, who were good and decent people, live. I said that I did not have an answer, but that we could turn the question and look at it another way. I believed that his parents, in their last dying moments, had prayed that their sons would live, and that at least for one son, my father, their prayer had come true. I didn't blame God for the Holocaust. I blamed the humans who turned their backs on God when they chose evil over goodness.

My parents wanted me to be untouched and untainted. But I believe that it is my responsibility to understand, to preserve and to impart this bitter legacy. I have great admiration for the survivors and gratitude for the liberators. I am brokenhearted and remain in mourning for the millions of victims. I could not change the past, but it did change me.

In the European and Jewish traditions, families were named for their line of work. An old family anecdote tells of how my father's lineage included salt merchants, hence his original name "Salzman," which is German for "Salt Man." At the beginning of this journey, all I knew of my father's past life was this name. And looking back like Lot's wife, and taking in the whole story, I could carry the pain of the Holocaust and find there is more to me than a pillar of salt.

GLOSSARY

Belzec. An extermination camp that operated from 1942 to 1943. Located in southeastern Poland, Belzec had an estimated 600,000 victims, almost all of them Jewish, making this camp one of the most deadly sites of Nazi murder. Jews from the surrounding towns and cities were brought in via railway, then sent immediately to the gas chambers. George Salton's family, along with the others from the Rzeszów ghetto, were sent to Belzec in July 1942. The camp was destroyed by the Germans in June of 1943 when there were no Jews left in the region to be killed.

Braunschweig. A satellite concentration camp that ran from 1944 to 1945 in central northern Germany. Braunschweig had 800 prisoners, most of them Jewish, who lived in huts and produced armaments for the Nazis. Nearly half died of hunger, illness, and maltreatment before the camp was closed in March 1945. Many of the remaining prisoners, including George Salton, were transferred to Wöbbelin, where they remained until they were liberated.

Flossenbürg. A concentration camp that operated between 1938 and 1945 at the eastern border of Nazi Germany. The camp housed political prisoners as well as Jews who labored in the stone quarry and later produced airplanes. Around 100,000 prisoners were held at Flossenbürg, of which approximately one-third died. George Salton was prisoner #16019 there. The camp was liberated by the Americans in April 1945.

Muselmen (or Muselmänner in German). A concentration camp slang term that refers to prisoners in a near-death state as a result of debilitating conditions. Many were pulled out during selections and sent to die, as they were unable to provide enough labor for the Nazis. A Muselman was recognized by the other prisoners as beyond help and hope.

Płaszów. Established as a forced labor camp in 1942, becoming a concentration camp in 1944. This camp, made famous by the film *Schindler's List*, was located outside of Kraków on the site of what used to be two Jewish cemeteries. Though the total number of prisoners held at Płaszów is not known, at any given time there were approximately 20,000 prisoners—mostly Jews—working there for German factories. The camp had no gas chambers; however, the Nazis carried out various forms of torture and mass shootings on its grounds. This was the camp where George Salton dug up old graves with his bare hands. Before the Soviet army arrived in January 1945, the Nazis demolished Płaszów.

Ravensbrück. A concentration camp, primarily for women and political prisoners, located in northern Germany. Ravensbrück functioned from 1939 to 1945. Approximately 130,000 female prisoners were held there, serving as subjects for medical experiments and providing slave labor for a German rocket manufacturer. In 1941 the Germans built next to Ravensbrück a small men's camp, where George Salton stayed between transits to other camps. In 1945 the Soviet Union liberated the camp.

Reichshof. A small labor camp at a German air factory in Rzeszów. It held thousands of prisoners, including hundreds of Jews from the Rzeszów ghetto and, later, from throughout Europe. Reichshof was operated by two German companies from 1939 to 1943, when the SS took control of the camp until its closure in 1944. The conditions were better and the death rate lower at Reichshof compared to that of other Nazi labor camps. This was the first concentration camp in which George Salton was imprisoned.

Rzeszów. City located in southeastern Poland that was occupied by the Germans in 1939 and where they created a ghetto in 1941. The Jewish population of Rzeszów was 15,000 before the war; it rose to 23,000 when Jews from the surrounding area, including George Salton and his family, were sent to the ghetto. In 1942 the Germans began to transport Jews from the Rzeszów ghetto to the Belzec extermination camp. In 1944 the few dozen Jews who remained in the Rzeszów ghetto were deported. Only 100 Jews originally from Rzeszów survived the Holocaust.

Sachsenhausen. A German concentration camp north of Berlin that was open from 1936 to 1945. Sachsenhausen initially held political prisoners, then other victims, such as Jews. Many of the camp's approximately 200,000 prisoners labored in its brickworks factory. Sachsenhausen had several satellite camps and a gas chamber. In April 1945 the Soviet and Polish armies liberated the camp.

Tomaszów Lubelski. A small town, and also the site of a ghetto, located near the Ukrainian border of eastern Poland. Tomaszów Lubelski, the hometown of Ruth Salton, had a Jewish population of about 6,000 (half of the whole population) before the Nazis invaded Poland in 1939. The ghetto they built was liquidated when all remaining Jews were sent on trucks to Belzec in October 1942. Many, including Ruth, were able to flee into the Russian zone of Poland and later crossed over into the Soviet Union for the duration of the war.

Tyczyn. A suburb of Rzeszów and the hometown of George Salton. Tyczyn is located in southeastern Poland. Before the war it had a Jewish population of about 1,000 (one-third of the whole town) and two synagogues. However, according to George Salton, it was "a small, old town without modern amenities, without a hospital, a library, a good restaurant or a hotel, without adequate shopping, or even a bank." In June 1941 the Jews of Tyczyn were sent to the nearby Rzeszów ghetto. By the end of the war, only a handful of Jews from Tyczyn had survived.

Urbès. A labor camp in eastern France at the German border. Urbès opened in August 1944 as an underground factory in a tunnel in the side of a mountain. There nearly 500 Jews labored for the German Air Force, creating engines for planes under the supervision of Daimler-Benz and the SS. The camp was evacuated in October 1944 due to the invasion of the Allies, and the prisoners, including George Salton, were transferred to Sachsenhausen.

Wannsee Conference. Organized by Reinhard Heydrich, this was a gathering of Nazi leadership that took place on January 20, 1942, in a house at Wannsee, near Berlin. Here the term "Final Solution of the Jewish Question" originated to describe the Third Reich's plan of systematically murdering the Jews of Europe through the use of death camps throughout Poland. Hitler had already approved of such measures by 1941, and the Wannsee Conference was intended to instruct German and Nazi officials, relevant government agencies, and the SS how to coordinate this Final Solution.

Watenstedt. A satellite camp of the Neuengamme concentration camp located in central Germany. Watenstedt opened in May 1944 and held 2,000 male prisoners, who labored for steel manufacturers. Prisoners lived in a series of huts surrounded by an electric barbed wire fence and were overseen by the SS. George Salton was at Watenstedt until April 1945, when the prisoners were transferred out.

Wieliczka. A labor camp in southern Poland, near Kraków. Wieliczka opened in March 1944 and held approximately 1,700 prisoners, many of them Jewish. Inmates worked on German military equipment in an underground factory set up in

Wieliczka's salt mine. The factory was dismantled because the Soviets approached before any manufacturing had commenced.

Wöbbelin. A subcamp of the Neuengamme concentration camp, constructed in September 1944 in northern Germany to house American prisoners of war. By February 1945, Wöbbelin expanded to include nearly 5,000 prisoners, many of them from other concentration camps, in an effort by the Nazis to keep them from being freed by the Allies. By the end of the war, no work was performed at the camp, food was scarce, and many prisoners died of starvation. The United States Army liberated Wöbbelin and its prisoners, including George Salton, on May 2, 1945. The locals of the nearby town of Ludwigslust were ordered by the US Army to visit the camp and publicly bury the dead.

ACKNOWLEDGMENTS

The manuscript for this book lay forgotten on a bookshelf after I abandoned any hope of completing this serious and personal work. My son, Aaron, having found and read the material, is largely responsible for its completion. I could not tell this story on my own, just as my father's book, *The 23rd Psalm*, benefitted from my support. Aaron, with his literary talent, encouragement, and commitment, breathed life into this project, and without him our family's story and my story would remain untold.

He shares a special bond with me and with my father that we call the "May 2nd Club." This was the date of my father's liberation, a miraculous event; it is also my birthday, which we have always celebrated along with his liberation. Also, it was on a May 2nd that Aaron survived a wreck in which his car was totaled by an eighteen-wheeler. Through all the difficulty in our lives, and in the aftermath of great tragedy, my father, my son, and I have persevered; we three generations of Jews have tried to honor our past and be thankful to God.

ABOUT THE AUTHORS

Anna Salton Eisen is the daughter of Holocaust survivor George Salton, and co-author with him of *The 23rd Psalm: A Holocaust Memoir*. She has conducted extensive research into the Holocaust and discovered many original documents that shed light on her father's experience. An active speaker, she is the subject of the documentary film *In My Father's Words*, about how her father and his fellow prisoners survived ten concentration camps in Poland, Germany, and France, and about her mission to find their descendants. She lives in Westlake, Texas.

Aaron Eisen is a third-generation Jewish writer. Along with co-authoring *Pillar of Salt,* he assisted in the production of *In My Father's Words*. A graduate of the University of Virginia and a resident of Dallas–Fort Worth, Texas, Aaron is working on a memoir about how the legacy of the Holocaust shaped his life and how the lessons of the Holocaust can help address an alarming breakdown in human connection and empathy.